DESTINED FOR SALVATION

God's Promise to Save Everyone

With best wishes,
Kalen Fristad

Also by Kalen Fristad:

DESTINED FOR SALVATION:
God's Promise to Save Everyone - Study Book,
For adults and youth, 13 lessons

To invite Rev. Fristad to speak to your church or group, or order copies of this book ($11.95; ten or more, $10.95) or the Study Book ($5.95; ten or more, $5.45), contact Destined For Salvation Ministries: P.O. Box 173, Newton, Iowa 50208, kkfristad@hotmail.com, www.destinedforsalvation.org, 319-899-3093.

DESTINED FOR SALVATION

God's Promise to Save Everyone

Kalen Fristad

Library of Congress Control Number: 2003092909

ISBN: 0-9729625-0-6

Second Printing August 2004

Scripture quotations, unless otherwise noted, are from the New
Revised Standard Version of the Bible, copyrighted in 1989 by the
Division of Christian Education of the National Council
of the Churches of Christ in the U.S.A.

Photo of Kalen Fristad on back cover by John Lee Photography.

Cover Photography Copyright © 1997 by Morris Press

Printed in the United States by Morris Publishing
3212 East Highway 30 • Kearney, NE 68847
1-800-650-7888

CONTENTS

PREFACE. IX

INTRODUCTION 1

Chapter 1: DARE TO POSSESS THE TRUTH:
What Does the Bible Say Regarding
Universal Salvation?. 6

Conflicting Biblical Voices, 7. A definition of
Salvation, 8. Scripture That Raises Questions About
Universal Salvation, 8. Scripture that Supports
Universal Salvation, 12. Making Our Decision, 16.

Chapter 2: SEEING THE BIGGER PICTURE:
General Biblical Themes .17

God's Quest to Save Us, 17. Judgment, 18. The
Grace of God, 21. The Purpose of Punishment or
Suffering, 23. God's Love, 25. Expiation, 26. Jesus'
Lack of Urgency, 27. Life After Death, 28.

Chapter 3: AMAZING GRACE:
Implications of Universal Salvation Versus
Eternal Damnation 31

God Is More Gracious Than Humans, 31. God Is
More Gracious Than Parents, 33. Gracious but Not
Soft on Sin, 35. Many Lack Opportunities to be
Saved, 35. Trying to Get God Off the Hook, 36.
Christ's Victory Is Complete, 37. A Joyous
Affirmation, 38.

Chapter 4: I WANT TO DO IT MYSELF:
Do We Have Free Will? 40

God Will Prevail, 41. Salvation for the Worst of
Sinners, 42. God Is Not a Monster, 42. Martin
Luther on Free Will, 43. The Idolatry of Free Will,
44. The Irresistible God, 45.

Chapter 5: LAYING A SOLID FOUNDATION:
What God Is Like 47

Family Deity, 48. Wizard Of Oz, 49. Spirit, 49.
Higher Power, 50. Oneness With Humankind, 52.
Ground of Our Being, 55. In Everything, 56.
Experienced Through Nature, 57. Love, 59. More
Thoughts about God, 60.

Chapter 6: FREE AT LAST:
From Hell to Heaven--How it is Accomplished . .63

Heaven and Hell - Spiritual States of Being, 63.
Change That Results in Heaven, 66. Original Sin -
Laziness, 66. There Is Hope, 68. Prepare For
Heaven, 68. The Command to Love, 69. About-
Face, 70.

Chapter 7: GOING BEYOND WISHFUL THINKING:
The Power of Unconditional Love. 73

Unconditional Love Is Essential, 73. Jesus'
Transforming Unconditional Love, 75. The Non-
judgmental Nature of God, 79. Risk and Power in
Following Jesus, 80. Passive and Assertive
Expressions of Unconditional Love, 84. Putting
Everything into God's Hands, 85. Unconditional
Love and Miracles, 86.

Chapter 8: FORGIVENESS IS ONLY THE BEGINNING:
Growing into God's Likeness. 89

Going Beyond Forgiveness, 89.   Healing, 90.
Becoming Fully Human, 91. Four Stages of Spiritual
Growth, 93. Don't Get Stuck in a Lower Spiritual
Stage, 94. Growth for Eternity, 97.

Chapter 9: MISERY LOVES COMPANY:
Why Some People Cling to the Idea of
Eternal Damnation 101

Negative Responses to the Good News, 101.
Verbalized Reasons for Opposing Universalism, 103.
Co-dependence, 104.   Co-dependence throughout
Church History, 106. Co-dependence Today, 109.

Chapter 10: THE ANCIENTS HAVE STOLEN OUR BEST IDEAS:
The History of Universalism 114

The Early Church, 114. Augustine, 117. Opposition
and Condemnation of Universalism, 119.   John
Wesley, 122. The American Colonies, 123. Feodor
Dostoevsky, 124.   Friedrich Schleiermacher, 125.
Dietrich Bonhoeffer, 125.   Karl Barth, 125.   Paul
Tillich, 125. A Long Rich History, 126.

Chapter 11: MAKING MOUNTAINS OUT OF MOUNTAINS:
The Significance of this Issue 128

Atheism, 128. Communism, 131. Pessimism, 131.
Satanism, 132. Lukewarm Christianity, 133. The
Unchurched, 134.   Unnecessary Agonizing, 135.
Meaninglessness and Meanness, 136.   Making the
World a Better Place, 137.   Loving Our Enemies,
139. Fear Versus Hope, 140. Bad News Versus
Good News, 141.   Jesus Said, "Let Your Light
Shine", 141.

Appendix: SILENCE IS NOT GOLDEN:
A Handbook on Spreading the Wonderful News
of Salvation for Everyone 143

Responses You Can Expect, 144. Utilizing
Opposition, 146. Hopefulness Through Faithful
Leadership, 148. The Blessing of Persecution, 149.

NOTES 151

PREFACE

I have written this book to let the world in on a secret that the Church has kept away from most people for the last 1,400 years. This is the secret: *God will eventually save everyone.* This truth, supported by the Bible, was widely accepted by early Christians for over 500 years. The belief in universal salvation was threatening to some Church leaders and the teaching was banished in the sixth century. In the eighteenth century, Christians once again began to affirm Universalism. Since then, many theologians, church leaders and millions of Christians have espoused it. God promises to save everyone, so there is hope for us all.

The hope of universal salvation stands in bold contrast to what many people claim to be good news. That is, God succeeds in saving those who have the good sense to become converted before death, but for the others, God throws them into hell and tosses away the key.

Thoughtful people are justified in rebelling against a God who would do such a thing. They seem to instinctively know that God is not condemning, but loving and saving. They consider the perception of the God of eternal damnation, as commonly taught by most Christian churches, to be incredibly bad news. The belief that God will not or cannot save everyone, and even imposes and enforces everlasting punishment, turns many people against God. That often results in spiritual tragedies, such as atheism, meaninglessness, meanness, and Satanism.

I too rebel against the teaching of a God of eternal damnation. Two of the most basic tenets of my faith are that God is unconditionally loving and is all-powerful. It is because of those two foundational beliefs and the specific support of universalism in the Bible that I am compelled to believe in it. A God who, out of love, desperately wants to save everyone but is unable to accomplish it, isn't much of a God. By the same token, a God who is quite capable of saving everyone but callously chooses to not do so is not much of a God. But the all-powerful and all-loving God as presented in the Scriptures, and in whom I believe, has enough love and power to save all of humankind.

This book is for those who are not content with the common teachings regarding God and everlasting punishment in hell, for those who are seeking more profound spiritual truth, and for those who are in outright rebellion against the Church, and even against God. I invite you to join me in exploring the issue of universalism and why it is so important for the people of today and will be for those in the generations to come.

INTRODUCTION

I was in seminary when Leslie Weatherhead (mid-twentieth century Church leader and pastor of City Temple, London) sparked my interest in the subject of universal salvation. In his book, *When the Lamp Flickers*, Weatherhead said Jesus taught that God would eventually save everyone. Weatherhead's premise held such a ring of truth and was so compelling that it set me off on a twenty-year journey of research, to learn everything I could about Universalism and why it is so important.

I learned that most people have never heard of the idea that God will eventually save everyone. Instead, they have been told throughout their lives that some people go to heaven and others go to hell. Without giving it much thought, most of them accept that conclusion.

When I tell people about universal salvation, their response is often quite favorable even though it is a new idea to most of them. A few people have given it much thought and have already rejected the idea of eternal damnation. They commonly respond with an enthusiastic expression of deep appreciation that someone finally articulated to them what they have always believed.

Universalism was a widely held belief during the early Church, has been espoused through the centuries by numerous theologians, and many people have always been receptive to it. I began to wonder why today so few people have heard that Universalism is grounded in biblical validity. And why is it that those who have come to believe in universal salvation through their own study or reasoning rarely speak up to let others know what they believe?

Speaking from my own personal experience as a minister, I have found that by making the slightest mention of it, I run the risk of experiencing judgment and wrath. Some people get quite upset and confrontational over the idea that God will eventually save everyone. They seem very threatened by it; tell me how wrong they think I am, and may even suggest that they believe I am so misguided I am in serious jeopardy of spending eternity in hell. No one wants to hear those damning words. I've learned over the years not to feel devastated by such attacks. Many people, however, choose to avoid the need to endure such severe criticism. As a result, most people who believe in universal salvation have been intimidated into silence.

Experiencing attacks from those who disagree with us shouldn't surprise us. After all, Jesus was also often severely criticized by those who saw things differently from him. But Jesus wasn't intimidated. He spoke freely of God's love, mercy, grace and forgiveness, and God's desire to save all people. Some self-righteous religious leaders (the scribes and Pharisees) believed Jesus was compromising the faith and leading people astray by portraying God as too loving and forgiving. After all, Jesus claimed that even notorious sinners such as prostitutes and tax collectors would be saved.

Jesus, in an encounter with the chief priests and the elders of the people who were not receptive to John the Baptist or himself, said, "Truly I tell you, the tax collectors and the prostitutes are going into the kingdom of God ahead of you" (Matthew 21:31). On another occasion, while Jesus "sat at dinner in the house, many tax collectors and sinners came and were sitting with him and his disciples. When the Pharisees saw this, they questioned his disciples, 'Why does your teacher eat with tax collectors and sinners?'" (Matthew 9:10-11).

The self-righteous begrudged God's generosity, mercy and forgiveness. In effect, they were saying, "How dare you accept the likes of those people, Jesus! We are much better than they. We have worked decades in faithful service to God, but you accept them as though they were just as good as us. It's not right! It's not fair! It's not just!"

In spite of what the scribes, Pharisees and others said, Jesus continued to preach and teach of God's limitless love, mercy, grace and forgiveness; illustrated in the parable of the Prodigal Son, according to Luke 15:11-32:

[11]Then Jesus said, "There was a man who had two sons. [12]The younger of them said to his father, 'Father, give me the share of the property that will belong to me.' So he divided his property between them. [13]A few days later the younger son gathered all he had and traveled to a distant country, and there he squandered his property in dissolute living. [14]When he had spent everything, a severe famine took place throughout that country, and he began to be in need. [15]So he went and hired himself out to one of the citizens of that country, who sent him to his fields to feed the pigs. [16]He would gladly have filled himself with the pods that the pigs were eating; and no one gave him anything. [17]But when he came to himself he said, 'How many of my father's hired hands have bread enough to spare, but here I am dying of hunger! [18]I will get up and go to my father, and I will say to him, "Father, I have sinned against heaven and before you; [19]I am no longer worthy to be called your son; treat me like one of your hired hands."' [20]So he set off and went to his father. But while he was still far off, his father saw him and was filled with compassion; he ran and put his arms around him and kissed him. [21]Then the son said to him,

'Father, I have sinned against heaven and before you; I am no longer worthy to be called your son.' [22]But the father said to his slaves, 'Quickly, bring out a robe—the best one—and put it on him; put a ring on his finger and sandals on his feet. [23]And get the fatted calf and kill it, and let us eat and celebrate; [24]for this son of mine was dead and is alive again; he was lost and is found!' And they began to celebrate.

[25]Now the elder son was in the field; and when he came and approached the house, he heard music and dancing. [26]He called one of the slaves and asked what was going on. [27]He replied, 'Your brother has come, and your father has killed the fatted calf, because he has got him back safe and sound.' [28]Then he became angry and refused to go in. His father came out and began to plead with him. [29]But he answered his father, 'Listen! For all these years I have been working like a slave for you, and I have never disobeyed your command; yet you have never given me even a young goat so that I might celebrate with my friends. [30]But when this son of yours came back, who has devoured your property with prostitutes, you killed the fatted calf for him!' [31]Then the father said to him, 'Son, you are always with me, and all that is mine is yours. [32]But we had to celebrate and rejoice, because this brother of yours was dead and has come to life; he was lost and has been found.'"

This parable captures perfectly the letter as well as the spirit of Jesus' teachings. What Jesus taught regarding unconditional love and acceptance of sinners is illustrated by the father accepting with open arms his wayward son. In the parable, the father represents God. This Scripture gives us confidence that God will eventually welcome into heaven not only those who remain faithful throughout their lives, as did the older son, but those who go astray as well.

The self-righteous religious leaders of Jesus' day could not accept much of what Jesus taught, and his close association with obvious sinners especially offended them. In an attempt to preserve the faith, as they understood it, they were highly critical of Jesus. That led to his crucifixion.

That same confrontation has continued ever since. Well-meaning people who see themselves as preservers of the true faith commonly criticize those who suggest that God will eventually save everyone. As a result, many people are intimidated into silence, and some turn away from the Christian faith, or even away from God, because they cannot accept the concept of a God of eternal damnation.

It has become very clear to me that it is true, and biblical, that God will eventually save everyone. We, therefore, must stand up for this great truth and speak out about it, even though it may subject us to the criticism of others.

In an attempt to do justice to this complex issue, we will consider it from various perspectives; beginning with what the Bible has to say.

Chapter One

DARE TO POSSESS THE TRUTH

What Does The Bible Say Regarding Universal Salvation?

It is a good thing to ask questions and struggle with what God would have us believe. We learn much from previous generations as well as our contemporaries, but if we never question what others have to tell us, our faith and knowledge will inevitably remain second-hand. We must raise questions and seek the truth for ourselves if what we know and believe is to become personal, alive, and powerful. God continually inspires and illuminates people through many means, such as Bible study and other reading, prayer, meditation, worship, the experience of nature, miracles, and interaction with others. Among the many sources of truth, I believe the Bible is the most important.

We put ourselves in jeopardy of not having well-founded beliefs if we accept a philosophy that runs contrary to the Bible. It is also important that we not blindly take someone else's word for what the Bible says, instead of reading the Word for ourselves. There can be multiple interpretations of Bible passages, so everyone will not readily agree on all points. What is most important is that we become knowledgeable of the Bible and trust God's truth as revealed to each of us. We should prayerfully submit ourselves to God's guidance in our quest for understanding each time we study the Bible.

We also risk failing to possess ultimate truth if we come to a conclusion prematurely or stubbornly cling to what we believe even when we have received information to the contrary. That reminds me of a favorite saying of a friend of mine; "Don't bother me with the facts. My mind is already made up." While it is sometimes unsettling to follow the truth wherever it might lead us, if we really want to grow and, indeed, possess the truth, that is what we must do.

I invite you to join me in a pursuit of the truth, as we realize there is much we do not know and could learn. With a humble and courageous attitude, may we be receptive to truth from all sources, even if it does not fit neatly into our present frame of reference.

Conflicting Biblical Voices

Have you ever noticed that the Bible sometimes seems to speak with more than one voice on a particular topic? In cases such as these, I know it can be hard for us to decide what we should believe. People who are knowledgeable of the Bible sometimes come to very different conclusions on any particular topic. In our differences as well as our agreements, I believe it is important that we relate to each other in a respectful manner. It is good for us to acknowledge that all interpretations and opinions are valid for discussion, especially if people have knowledge of the Bible and seek to support their ideas with God's teachings.

The Bible seems to speak in multiple voices with regard to God's universal grace. Some passages seem to suggest that if a person is to be saved, conversion must take place in this life because following death, one goes either to heaven or hell, to stay for eternity. Other passages indicate that God will eventually save everyone, including those initially condemned to hell.

When we study the Bible to discern the truth of universal salvation, it is evident that we cannot rely on only one or two passages of Scripture to reach our conclusions. We must consider all relevant passages on both sides of this issue. We will also need to let some general themes in the Bible speak to us as we seek to determine what it really says regarding whether or not everyone will eventually be saved.

A Definition of Salvation

Salvation is what this book is all about. I believe salvation is best defined in the words of Jesus where he says, "For God so loved the world that he gave his only Son, so that everyone who believes in him may not perish but may have eternal life" (John 3:16).

Believing in Christ involves two things: 1) Humbly admitting our shortcomings and sins to God and repenting of them. 2) Making a commitment to faithfully serve Christ (God) and allowing God to transform us so we may become more like God in our love and faithfulness. Believing in Christ is sometimes referred to as being converted (turned around), born again (or born of the Spirit, or from above), or accepting Christ as our Savior.

Regardless of what we call it, it is important for us to realize that salvation is not just a one-time event but is an ongoing experience. The initial acceptance of salvation puts us on the right track, but that is only the beginning. The apostle Paul makes reference to this ongoing process in 1 Corinthians 1:18, where he writes of those of us "who are being saved." Much of what I say in this book will relate to salvation as this continuing experience of transformation and growth.

Scripture That Raises Questions
About Universal Salvation

Let's consider some passages that indicate that the unsaved will experience hell following death and that there may not be chances for conversion in the next life. They are as follows:
1. Matthew 13:24-30, 36-43
Jesus told a parable of a man who sowed good seed in his field, but an enemy sowed weeds among the man's wheat.

Rather than pulling the weeds and risking uprooting the wheat at the same time, the man told his slaves, "³⁰Let both of them grow together until the harvest; and at harvest time I will tell the reapers, Collect the weeds first and bind them in bundles to be burned, but gather the wheat into my barn." Jesus' disciples asked him to explain the parable to them. He responded;

> "³⁷The one who sows the good seed is the Son of Man; ³⁸the field is the world, and the good seed are the children of the kingdom; the weeds are the children of the evil one, ³⁹and the enemy who sowed them is the devil; the harvest is the end of the age, and the reapers are angels. ⁴⁰Just as the weeds are collected and burned up with fire, so will it be at the end of the age. ⁴¹The Son of Man will send his angels, and they will collect out of his kingdom all causes of sin and all evildoers, ⁴²and they will throw them into the furnace of fire, where there will be weeping and gnashing of teeth. ⁴³Then the righteous will shine like the sun in the kingdom of their Father. Let anyone with ears listen!"

This passage makes it very clear that hell is terrible and that it will be experienced by the unsaved following death. It does not indicate that hell is without end.

2. Matthew 25:1-13

Jesus said that the kingdom of heaven will be like ten bridesmaids who took their lamps to meet the bridegroom. Five of them were wise and brought extra oil for their lamps, but the others foolishly neglected to do so. The bridegroom was so long in arriving that the lamps of the foolish bridesmaids began to run out of oil. While they were gone to buy more oil, "¹⁰the bridegroom came, and those who were ready went with him into the wedding banquet; and the door was shut. ¹¹Later the other bridesmaids came also, saying, 'Lord, lord, open to us.' ¹²But he replied, 'Truly I tell you, I do not know you.' ¹³Keep awake therefore, for you know neither the day nor the hour."

The bridegroom in this case represents Christ, the wedding banquet is heaven and the shutting of the door refers to death. It is tragic to be left out, so everyone is well advised to be ready to meet God at any time. Again, however, this passage gives no indication that finding oneself excluded from the wedding banquet is a permanent situation.

3. Matthew 25:31-46

Jesus said that when he returns he will sit on his throne and the people of all nations will be gathered before him, with the righteous on the right hand side and the unrighteous on the left. Then he "[34]will say to those at his right hand, 'Come, you that are blessed by my Father, inherit the kingdom prepared for you from the foundation of the world,'" because of the many ways they had faithfully helped others and, in so doing, served him. To those at his left hand, however, he will say "[41]'You that are accursed, depart from me into the eternal fire prepared for the devil and his angels,'" because they had failed to serve anyone but themselves. He concludes by saying, "[46]these will go away into eternal punishment, but the righteous into eternal life."

This passage, along with rest of the New Testament, was written in Greek. In order to understand the passage, it is very helpful to consider the meaning of the Greek word that is translated "eternal." While a study of this may seem initially confusing, it will shed great light on this topic.

The Greek word *aionios*, translated "eternal" does not necessarily apply only to the length of life. It is used in the Bible in reference to the quality of life, to accent the wonderful joy of heaven or the terrible misery of hell. Jesus says in a prayer, "This is eternal life, that they may know you, the only true God, and Jesus Christ whom you have sent" (John 17:3).

Secondly, the English words "eternal" and "everlasting" both mean "without end," but the Greek words from which they are a translation don't have exactly the same meaning. Greek is a much richer language in some respects than English. There is more than one Greek word that translates as "eternal" or "everlasting" in English.

If the writers of the New Testament had intended to communicate the concept of punishment without end, they could have used the word *aidios*, (meaning perpetual[1]) but they didn't. *Aidios* is used only twice in the New Testament; in

Romans 1:20, where reference is made to God's "eternal power and deity," and in Jude 6, which refers to fallen angels being kept "in eternal chains... until the judgment." Instead of using *aidios* the writers chose *aionios*. *Aionios* appears 68 times in the New Testament, and is translated "eternal," "everlasting" or "forever." In 51 of those 68 times *aionios* is used in reference to fire (of hell), life, punishment, destruction, damnation or judgment.[2]

Some people interpret *aionios* as meaning "without end." But many early Christian scholars for whom Greek was their mother tongue (such as Origen of Alexandria) believed that *aionios* meant, "indefinite but limited duration"[3] rather than "without end." A Greek English lexicon defines *aionios* as, "lasting for an age."[4] *Young's Analytical Concordance to the Bible* gives *aionios* the definition, "age lasting."[5] "Age lasting" would not mean the same as "without end," but would last to the end of the age, however long that might be. By virtue of the definition of *aionios*, therefore, we can conclude that eternal punishment in hell will eventually come to an end.

4. Luke 16:19-31

Jesus told the following parable:

> [19]"There was a rich man who was dressed in purple and fine linen and who feasted sumptuously every day. [20]And at his gate lay a poor man named Lazarus, covered with sores, [21]who longed to satisfy his hunger with what fell from the rich man's table; even the dogs would come and lick his sores. [22]The poor man died and was carried away by the angels to be with Abraham. The rich man also died and was buried. [23]In Hades, where he was being tormented, he looked up and saw Abraham far away with Lazarus by his side. [24]He called out, 'Father Abraham, have mercy on me, and send Lazarus to dip the tip of his finger in water and cool my tongue; for I am in agony in these flames.' [25]But Abraham said, 'Child, remember that during your lifetime you received your good things, and Lazarus in like manner evil things; but now he is comforted here,

and you are in agony. [26]Besides all this, between you and us a great chasm has been fixed, so that those who might want to pass from here to you cannot do so, and no one can cross from there to us.' [27]He said, 'Then, father, I beg you to send him to my father's house— [28]for I have five brothers—that he may warn them, so that they will not also come into this place of torment.' [29]Abraham replied, 'They have Moses and the prophets; they should listen to them.' [30]He said, 'No, father Abraham; but if someone goes to them from the dead, they will repent.' [31]He said to him, 'If they do not listen to Moses and the prophets, neither will they be convinced even if someone rises from the dead.'"

It is helpful to realize that each parable that Jesus told is meant to communicate primarily one main lesson. This parable regarding the rich man and Lazarus should not be considered an actual description of hades (hell) and heaven, including things such as a chasm that cannot be crossed. Rather, it communicates the understanding that those who make riches their god, and practice self-indulgence, will surely experience hell. I'll discuss this passage at greater length in chapter six.

5. 2 Thessalonians 1:5-9

In this passage, the Apostle Paul states that, as evidence of God's righteous judgment, when Jesus returns from heaven he will inflict "[8]vengeance on those who do not know God and on those who do not obey the gospel of our Lord Jesus. [9]These will suffer the punishment of eternal destruction, separated from the presence of the Lord and from the glory of his might." This passage of Scripture, along with the others I have quoted above, apparently supports the idea of hell in the next life, but there are legitimate reasons to conclude that, for an individual, hell is not necessarily without end.

Scripture That Supports Universal Salvation

Many Bible passages suggest everyone will eventually be saved. Some present the concept that God will even save people from hell. These passages need to be considered before we can each make an informed decision regarding what we should believe about universal salvation. Some of these passages are as follows:

1. Matthew 18:21-22

Peter asked Jesus, "[21]'Lord, if another member of the church sins against me, how often should I forgive? As many as seven times?' [22]Jesus said to him, 'Not seven times, but, I tell you, seventy-seven times.'" In other words, Jesus tells us there should be no end to our willingness to forgive others. Is it reasonable to think that God's forgiveness is limited? Is God less forgiving than God expects us to be? Surely not!

Indeed, that is the meaning of the cross. Twentieth century Scottish theologian, William Barclay, wrote, "If Jesus had refused or escaped the Cross, if he had not died, it would have meant that there was some point in suffering and sorrow at which the love of God stopped, that there was some point beyond which forgiveness was impossible. But the Cross is God saying in Jesus: 'There is no limit to which my love will not go and no sin which my love cannot forgive.'"[6]

2. Luke 15:3-6

Jesus told this parable: "[4]'Which one of you, having a hundred sheep and losing one of them, does not leave the ninety-nine in the wilderness and go after the one that is lost until he finds it? [5]When he has found it, he lays it on his shoulders and rejoices. [6]And when he comes home, he calls together his friends and neighbors, saying to them, 'Rejoice with me, for I have found my sheep that was lost.'" In this parable, the shepherd (God) wasn't content with 99 percent of his flock being saved, but looked for the one lost sheep until he found it. That resulted in great rejoicing. For God to stop looking for the lost sheep is to stop being God (love).

3. John 12:32

Jesus said, "I, when I am lifted up from the earth, will draw all people to myself." Being "lifted up from the earth" is a reference to Jesus' crucifixion, through which he will draw all people to himself (that is, save everyone).

4. John 12:46-47

Jesus stated, "⁴⁶'I have come as light into the world, so that everyone who believes in me should not remain in the darkness. ⁴⁷I do not judge anyone who hears my words and does not keep them, for I came not to judge the world, but to save the world.'" Jesus came to save everyone in the world!

5. Romans 5:18

Paul the apostle wrote, "Therefore just as one man's trespass led to condemnation for all, so one man's act of righteousness leads to justification and life for all." Adam is the first man referred to in this passage. The Bible teaches us that it was the result of his sin that sin was introduced into the world and all of humankind came to experience sinfulness, and thus condemnation. The second man refers to Christ. It was through his act of righteousness (willingly dying on the cross for the sins of humankind) that leads to salvation for all. A passage similar to this is found in 1 Corinthians 15:22, where Paul writes, "For as all die in Adam, so all will be made alive in Christ."

6. Romans 8:38-39

Paul proclaimed, "³⁸For I am convinced that neither death, nor life, nor angels, nor rulers, nor things present, nor things to come, nor powers, ³⁹nor height, nor depth, nor anything else in all creation, will be able to separate us from the love of God in Christ Jesus our Lord." Since nothing, including death can separate us from the love of God, it is hard to imagine God not seeking release from hell for the people God loves.

7. Philippians 2:10-11

Paul wrote, "¹⁰At the name of Jesus every knee should bend, in heaven and on earth and under the earth, ¹¹and every tongue should confess that Jesus Christ is Lord." The phrase "under the earth" is a clear reference to the abode of the dead or hell. To "confess that Jesus Christ is Lord" was a phrase used in early baptismal services by which those being baptized expressed their commitment to Christ or declared that they had been saved through Christ.[7] To say that everyone under the earth (in hell) should bend their knee (bow humbly before Christ) and confess that Jesus Christ is Lord (profess salvation through Christ) is to affirm that it is possible for those in hell to be saved and that everyone in hell will eventually experience salvation.

8. 1 Peter 3:18-20; 4:6

The author of the first letter of Peter writes:

> [18]For Christ also suffered for sins once for all, the righteous for the unrighteous, in order to bring you to God. He was put to death in the flesh, but made alive in the spirit, [19]in which also he went and made a proclamation to the spirits in prison, [20]who in former times did not obey. . . .[6]For this is the reason the gospel was proclaimed even to the dead, so that, though they had been judged in the flesh as everyone is judged, they might live in the spirit as God does.

This passage makes a clear and specific reference to Jesus saving people from hell.

9. Colossians 1:19-20

Paul declared regarding Christ, "[19]For in him all the fullness of God was pleased to dwell, [20]and through him God was pleased to reconcile to himself all things, whether on earth or in heaven, by making peace through the blood of his cross." The necessity of reconciliation presupposes estrangement between God and all things. God was not content with things as they were, so God sent Jesus to rescue humanity. The good news is that God, through Christ, was pleased to reconcile to himself all things, including all humans.

10. 1 Timothy 2:4-6

Paul proclaimed, "[4](God) desires everyone to be saved and to come to the knowledge of the truth. [5]For there is one God; there is also one mediator between God and humankind, Jesus Christ, himself human, [6]who gave himself a ransom for all." Surely we can agree that God gets what God wants, since God is all-powerful. An affirmation of this truth is found in Job 42:1-2; "Then Job answered the Lord: 'I know that you can do all things, and that no purpose of yours can be thwarted.'" Also Ephesians 1:11 reads, "In Christ we have also obtained an inheritance, having been destined according to the purpose of him who accomplishes all things according to his council and will." God is not a weakling. If God desires everyone to be saved, will God not succeed?

11. 1 John 2:1-2

The disciple, John, wrote, "[1]My little children, I am writing these things to you so that you may not sin. But if anyone does sin, we have an advocate with the Father, Jesus Christ the righteous; [2]and he is the atoning sacrifice for our sins, and not for ours only but also for the sins of the whole world." The reference, "not for ours only" indicates that Jesus' atoning sacrifice was not just for a select group, but was for everyone.

Making Our Decision

There are passages of Scripture on both sides of the issue of universal salvation. There are numerous additional relevant passages, which may be helpful to us in our quest to discern the truth, but I believe the ones I have set out above are most significant. A review of these Scripture passages may not necessarily lead a person to conclude that one side or the other is correct. It may just cause confusion. Or individuals may arrive at opposite conclusions about God eventually saving everyone.

What are we to do when we find apparently conflicting passages in the Bible? How does one decide what is correct when there seems to be biblical support for both sides related to the question of universal salvation? To help us work through the confusion and discern the truth, there are many general biblical themes and profound implications that we need to consider. We will do that in the next two chapters.

Chapter Two

SEEING THE BIGGER PICTURE

General Biblical Themes

To really understand what the Bible says it is sometimes necessary to go beyond looking at individual passages such as we have done in the last chapter. It's often very helpful to look for general themes in the Bible that relate to a particular issue. Certainly there are several general themes that are relevant to the issue of universal salvation versus eternal damnation.

God's Quest to Save Us

The most dominant and basic theme of the Bible is God's quest to save people. Evidence of that first shows up in the book of Genesis, chapter three. It was after Adam and Eve were tempted by the serpent and ate of the forbidden fruit. God said to the serpent, "I will put enmity between you and the woman, and between your offspring and hers; he will strike your head and you will strike his heel" (Genesis 3:15). This verse is commonly understood to be the first prediction of a Messiah to be sent to save humankind; the Messiah being the offspring of the woman, with the offspring of the serpent representing Satan. Striking "his heel" is in reference to the crucifixion as Satan's effort to defeat the Messiah. Paradoxically, the crucifixion along with the resurrection was

God's way of striking a blow to the head of Satan. Through what seemed initially to be the most tragic of all events, God provided salvation for the world and hope for life after death.

The theme of God's quest to save us is evident in many places throughout the Bible. God inspired prophets to call all people into a faithful relationship with God, as is expressed in Jeremiah 3:22, "Return, O faithless children, I will heal your faithlessness."

Jesus continues the theme by saying, "The Spirit of the Lord is upon me, because he has anointed me to bring good news to the poor. He has sent me to proclaim release to the captives and recovery of sight to the blind, to let the oppressed go free, to proclaim the year of the Lord's favor" (Luke 4:18-19). Jesus called his disciples and other followers to carry on his work. His parting words to them were, "You will receive power when the Holy Spirit has come upon you; and you will be my witnesses in Jerusalem, in all Judea and Samaria, and to the ends of the earth" (Acts 1:8).

Judgment

Another theme which runs through the Bible is judgment, referred to in Hebrews 9:27; "It is appointed for mortals to die once, and after that the judgment." I believe the judgment scene is never one of a judge sitting on a throne who tells a trembling sinner that he or she is hell-bound, and informs others they are destined for heaven. Instead, we judge ourselves through our conscience in the light of God's love and mercy.

This understanding of judgment is reflected in Raymond A. Moody Jr.'s books, *Life After Life* and *Reflections on Life After Life*. He relates the many testimonies of people who had experienced clinical death and were later revived. Their experiences were remarkably similar in detail. Among many other things, those with near-death experiences commonly reported experiencing an encounter with a being of light. They felt total and unconditional love and acceptance from this being of light whom many people identified as Christ. Moody writes, "The love and the warmth which emanate from this being to the dying person are utterly beyond words, and he feels completely surrounded by it and taken up in it, completely at ease and accepted in the presence of this being. He senses an irresistible magnetic attraction to this light."[1]

The being of light asked them questions, not in condemnation or accusation, but in a manner that helped them think about their lives. As a result, Moody discovered, "a kind of judgment took place, for in this state of heightened awareness, when people saw any selfish acts which they had done they felt extremely repentant. Likewise, when gazing upon those events in which they had shown love and kindness they felt satisfaction. It is interesting to note that the judgment in the cases I studied came not from the being of light, who seemed to love and accept these people anyway, but rather from within the individual being judged."[2]

The idea that people judge themselves is also represented in John 3:19-21, where Jesus is quoted as saying, "And this is the judgment, that the light has come into the world, and people loved darkness rather than light because their deeds were evil. For all who do evil hate the light and do not come to the light, so that their deeds may not be exposed. But those who do what is true come to the light, so that it may be clearly seen that their deeds have been done in God." This passage makes it clear to me that people themselves will decide whether they go to the light or darkness (heaven or hell). But I want to make it very clear that if someone chooses to go to hell, it is not a final choice. I believe God will not let it be so. It is not as if people have complete free will, that whatever they choose is acceptable to God and will stand forever.

I will address the issue of free will in depth in chapter four, but for now let us affirm that people do have some freedom to choose heaven or hell. That means that judgment is not simply a matter of God analyzing how people have lived their lives, welcoming some into heaven and throwing others into hell against their will. It also leaves open the possibility of God leading people from hell to heaven, once they have "seen the light".

I'm convinced Jesus understood judgment as a beginning, not as an end. Therefore, rather than focusing on the past, our attention should be on the future. Judgment must no longer be thought of as the last crushing word on a failed life, but the first word of invitation to a new one. Jesus made this new life a reality for people whom the religious establishment considered outcasts and deemed unacceptable to God. Instead of waiting for them to repent, Jesus declared that those outcasts were forgiven. This motivated them to repent and accept salvation from God.

We tend to be less sympathetic of others when their suffering is something they have brought on themselves. For example, if we hear of a drunk driver who was involved in an accident that resulted in injuries to him, rather than showing compassion we might say, "He had it coming. He got what he deserved." With that attitude, we may have reluctantly gone to his aid if we had been on the scene. If an innocent person was injured in the accident, however, we naturally assume we would have responded quickly and done whatever we could to help him.

Sadly, it seems that the same is true of how we think about people who might be experiencing hell in the next life. If a strong minded person has very deservedly gotten himself into hell by deliberately living an evil life, some of us may conclude that it is perfectly all right for him to suffer in hell forever. On the other hand, a weaker person may be in hell because of being led astray by the wrong crowd. With someone like that, most of us would be inclined to hope that God would somehow rescue him from his living hell because he really didn't deserve it.

Our task is to move beyond judging people and assessing whether they deserve our compassion. Just as "God shows no partiality" (Romans 2:11), may that become true of each of us. The truth of the matter is, we are all sinners. We all deserve to experience hell because it is a direct consequence of sin. By the same token, none of us deserves to experience the joy of heaven because we have all sinned. We are admitted into the fullness of heaven only by the grace of God. Because of God's grace no one can be consigned to the misery of hell forever even though we may believe he very much deserves it.

Could heaven truly be heavenly for anyone if even one soul is forever forbidden from entering it? Even if being in hell is that person's own fault? There would always be a lingering sadness over those who were absent, who would never have a chance to experience the joys of heaven. If someone is in an accident and it is entirely his own fault, you don't refuse to take him to the hospital to be treated, do you? In the infinitely more important matter relating to a person's eternal welfare the same principle must surely apply. No matter how much the fault is our own (and to some extent it always is) the love of God will never cease trying to win us.

The Grace of God

The concept of God's grace is one of the most dominant themes in the Bible. Grace is commonly defined as unmerited favor. Try as we might, we can never achieve God's standard of holiness and perfection, but God accepts and loves us anyway. This is expressed in Psalms 103:8,10,12; "[8]The Lord is merciful and gracious, slow to anger and abounding in steadfast love. . . . [10]He does not deal with us according to our sins, nor repay us according to our iniquities. . . . [12]as far as the east is from the west, so far he removes our transgressions from us."

Ephesians 2:8-9 reads: "[8]For by grace you have been saved through faith, and this is not your own doing; it is the gift of God - [9]not the result of works, so that no one may boast." If we insist that people must respond favorably to the gospel before they die in order to be saved, we have concluded that the grave is the end point of God's grace. It is clear to me that one cannot make a very convincing argument for that conclusion. It seems rather, in the words of David Lowes Watson, author of *God Does Not Foreclose,* that "if persons are to be tried in an eternal court for neglecting to respond to the gospel as it is regularly proclaimed and demonstrated by the average North

American congregation, any competent defense lawyer would immediately, and successfully, appeal. Which is, of course, precisely what Christ does for us in eternity."[3] Listen to what the Bible says according to Romans 8:34; "Who is to condemn? It is Christ Jesus, who died, yes, who was raised, who is at the right hand of God, who indeed intercedes for us."

We can never wear down the grace of God. God's grace remains no matter what sins we commit. Jesus illustrates God's grace very well in the parable of the Prodigal Son (Luke 15:11-32), where the father remained steadfast in his love and acceptance despite his son's mistakes. When the son returned to him it was clear that the father was redemptive, compassionate, and concerned. No matter what the son had done, his father never failed to give his grace and love to him. The father did not resort to punishment. Instead, he ran to his son and kissed him, demonstrating the strength of their bond. When the young man left home, he had not ceased to be his father's son, as he had feared. Therefore, when he returned to his father, there was no need for his sonship to be reinstated. Instead, his father expressed loving forgiveness and acceptance. The son's eyes were opened, and he became aware of the father/son relationship that had always existed between them.

What this means is that God does not hold a grudge. Neither does God require us to do a prescribed amount of groveling before granting forgiveness. God does not demand justice. When we turn to God, we are accepted immediately and unconditionally because God has already acted in Christ to receive us. It is God, who by grace draws us to Godself, so how can we entertain, even for a moment, the thought that God may be reluctant or slow to forgive us? God doesn't wait until we have paid the price, until we have been punished for our sins, before accepting us. Certainly, we experience the misery we have brought upon ourselves as a consequence of our behavior. But can you truly call that God's doing? God accepts us and welcomes us home without regard for what we have done in the past, just as did the father in the story of the Prodigal Son.

"While he was still far off, his father saw him and was filled with compassion; he ran and put his arms around him and kissed him. . . . 'Let us eat and celebrate; for this son of mine was dead and is alive again; he was lost and is found'" (Luke 15: 20, 23-24).

Many people place a great deal of emphasis on the idea of justice, or the assumed rewards and punishments given by God. This idea gives more credence to justice than grace. Wouldn't it be arrogant of us to believe that a holy and just God, one who must punish sin, would let us go to heaven while condemning others to hell? If God operated strictly on the basis of justice, no one would be acceptable.

The good news of the Christian gospel is that no one goes to heaven except by grace, and that no one is so bad as to be beyond the possibility of experiencing salvation by grace. For God to let any of us in to heaven at all, while Jesus died to provide salvation for us, is the ultimate injustice, for Jesus was without sin. It is important not to place undue emphasis on the idea of the justice of God. I believe we need to move away from the concept of justice, or reward and punishment. No one can do anything so bad that God's grace is exhausted to the extent God becomes angry and punishing. Those things that we experience that seem to be rewards or punishments do not come from God. They are the natural consequences of behavior, whether that be the misery caused by wrongdoing, or the happiness, healing and joy which results from doing what is right.

The Purpose of Punishment or Suffering

Considering the natural consequences of our actions leads us to examine the biblical theme regarding the purpose of punishment or suffering.

In an attempt to support their belief of endless punishment in hell, some people will say, "God is holy, and for that reason the punishment of evildoers is a moral necessity." In reality, while that may seem proper and just, the Bible presents us with an even higher standard. It teaches us that the ultimate moral necessity is that people be converted through punishment or suffering.

One example in the Bible that illustrates this is found in the book of Jeremiah. The Babylonians had conquered the Israelites and many of them had been taken to Babylonia as slaves. The explanation for why that had happened is found in Jeremiah 9:13-16; "[13]The Lord says: Because they have forsaken my law that I set before them, and have not obeyed my voice, or walked in accordance with it, [14]but have stubbornly followed their own hearts and have gone after the Baals, as their ancestors taught them. [15]Therefore thus says the Lord of hosts, the God of Israel: . . . [16]I will scatter them among nations that neither they nor their ancestors have known."

God was not content, however, that the Israelites had merely gotten what they deserved for their disloyalty. Instead, God wanted them to return so they could be healed, as is expressed in Jeremiah 3:12-13, 22; "[12]Return, faithless Israel, says the Lord. I will not look on you in anger, for I am merciful, says the Lord; I will not be angry forever. [13]Only acknowledge your guilt, that you have rebelled against the Lord your God. [22]Return, O faithless children, I will heal your faithlessness." The completion of this redemptive process is affirmed by God in Jeremiah 32:37-38; "[37]See, I am going to gather them from all the lands to which I drove them in my anger and my wrath and in great indignation; I will bring them back to this place, and I will settle them in safety. [38]They shall be my people, and I will be their God."

These passages taken together accent the biblical truths that the reason for punishment or suffering is to bring about conversion, and that God has unlimited capacity to forgive those who turn to God. God allowed the Babylonians to conquer and enslave the Israelites for the purpose of getting the Israelites to return to God, to convert them from following the Baals (false gods), and once again live in a faithful manner.

The purpose of biblical punishment is to make a wrongdoer a right-doer. If hell is endured without end, the experience would be of no value to an individual because there would be no chance of his embracing good, repenting and attempting a new beginning. Such a circumstance would be a travesty. Suffering from which nothing can be learned or gained is meaningless, and the one who brought it about would be a fiend, not a father. We as parents discipline our children, not for the sake of punishment, but in order to encourage change. Surely God is at least as honorable as any parent in this regard.

According to the Bible then, punishment (more specifically, suffering which we bring on ourselves as a direct consequence of our behavior) is never an end in itself, but is a means to bring about conversion. So we can properly conclude that hell has a useful purpose, whether it's the hell that we experience in this life or in the next. Its purpose is to help us realize the futility, hopelessness and meaninglessness of life without God. It helps us realize our need for God to save us. The ultimate end is not for God to punish sin but to eliminate the sin and, through conversion and transformation, save the sinner.

God's Love

What could be a more important theme in the Bible than God's love? 1 John 3:7-9 declares, "Beloved, let us love one another, because love is from God; everyone who loves is born of God and knows God. Whoever does not love does not know God, for God is love. God's love was revealed among us in this way: God sent his only Son into the world so that we might live through him."

The belief that God is love presents serious difficulties for those who also believe in endless punishment in hell. Once they think about it, not surprisingly, they confront a natural difficulty in reconciling the idea of a God whose love is limitless and unending, with the idea of a God who callously permits and even enforces endless punishment.

One way out of their dilemma is to conclude that God's love is limited and conditional. For example, they may contend that God's love is of two basic kinds--complacent or benevolent. Complacent love, according to them, is mandatory.

It is love for someone who is morally upright. God would be obligated to love someone like Jesus, or a saint, for instance. On the other hand, they believe benevolent love is optional (the love for one who is not praiseworthy or righteous, that is, someone who is unworthy of love). With this way of thinking, they might decide that because people in hell are not praiseworthy, God has no obligation to love them. Though they accept that God is love, to them it does not seem necessary for God to love people who are in hell.

It's hard for me to comprehend how anyone could believe that God's love is optional. After all, the essence of God's grace is to love the unlovable, and forgive us even though we don't deserve it. To believe that God's love is limited and conditional is, in a sense, to make God into our own image. Even worse, it results in lowering God's status below humans. Humans have the ability to love those who are not worthy of love, and because of Christian teachings, feel somewhat of an obligation to do so. It is absurd to think that God could be less loving than humans.

Expiation

Another of the Biblical themes, and one of its most powerful, is expiation. Expiation relates to the means by which atonement or reparation is made. We as humans are not able to make atonement for ourselves, so another way had to be provided. The Jews had come to believe that a sacrificial lamb made atonement. The New Testament takes us beyond that line of thinking with the advent of Jesus the Messiah. The significance of the Christian teaching regarding expiation is not that a Messiah, separate from God, made atonement for us. It was God who came to our rescue. God did not wait for us to demonstrate that we were worthy of God's love and salvation. Romans 5:8 reads, "God proves his love for us in that while we still were sinners Christ died for us."

Christ's death was not for the purpose of appeasing an angry God. Such an act would be pagan. Pagans in ancient times sometimes sacrificed their children to appease the angry god they feared. The Christian teaching is that we no longer need to try to appease God because it was God through Christ who provided the means for our salvation. Consequently, we can affirm that the need is not to reconcile God to us, but to reconcile ourselves to God. God does not need to be appeased. It is we humans who need to be changed.

John 3:16 reads, "For God so loved the world that he gave his only Son, so that everyone who believes in him may not perish but may have eternal life." And in 2 Corinthians 5:19 we read, "In Christ God was reconciling the world to himself, not counting their trespasses against them." 1 John 4:10 reads, "In this is love, not that we loved God but that he loved us and sent his Son to be the atoning sacrifice (expiation) for our sins."

At Christmas time, we talk and sing about "Emmanuel", which means "God is with us." This suggests that Jesus did not come to die on the cross in order to appease an angry God. It was God himself who came to save us. According to Isaiah 53:5, "He was wounded for our transgressions, crushed for our iniquities; upon him was the punishment that made us whole, and by his bruises we are healed."

Never again should we think of God as an angry God whom we must try to appease. God doesn't look for reasons to condemn us. God never gives up looking for ways to get us to stop resisting so God can save us. Consistent with the expiation theme, in John 3:17, Jesus says, "Indeed, God did not send the Son into the world to condemn the world, but in order that the world might be saved through him." What good news that is!

Jesus' Lack of Urgency

If Jesus believed the unsaved were destined to go to hell forever, I believe there would have been much greater urgency reflected in his ministry. I do not detect that kind of urgency in Jesus as I read about him in the Bible. He does not appear to frantically emphasize the importance of people getting saved before they die. There were many times people turned away from Jesus, and he let them go. For example, on one occasion a rich young man asked Jesus what he must do to have eternal life. Jesus told him to sell his possessions, give the money to the poor and to follow him. The young man "went away grieving, for he had many possessions" (Matthew 19:22). On another occasion, because of a dispute over Jesus' claim to be the bread of life, "many of his (followers) turned back and no longer went about with him" (John 6:66).

There is no indication that Jesus ever ran down the road after anyone to get him or her saved. He displayed unhurried patience, as if he had a lot of time. That kind of attitude is reflected in 2 Peter 3:8-9 which reads, "But do not ignore this one fact, beloved, that with the Lord one day is like a thousand years, and a thousand years is like one day. The Lord is not slow about his promise, as some think of slowness, but is patient with you, not wanting any to perish, but all to come to repentance."

Jesus exhibited patience and a lack of urgency, but that doesn't mean what he was doing wasn't important. His mission was so significant he was willing to die for the cause. According to Luke 19:41, Jesus "wept over (the city of Jerusalem)" because so many people there had gone astray. Also, he said there is great "joy in heaven over one sinner who repents" (Luke 15:7). The good news Jesus came to offer us is extremely significant, yet in spite of its importance, Jesus showed no urgency to get people saved before they died. His patience suggests he believed he had all of time to accomplish his mission. If people did not begin to follow him before death, there would be plenty of opportunities for them to see the light in the life to come.

Life after Death

While the Bible is not generous with details about life after death, it is still obviously an important theme. Many people hold to the belief that the devil is in hell with those who are lost, and God (Father, Son and Holy Spirit) is in heaven with those who are saved, and that arrangement will continue for eternity. John 14:2-3 seems to support this belief. It quotes Jesus as saying, "In my Father's house there are many dwelling places. If it were not so, would I have told you that I go to prepare a place for you? And if I go and prepare a place for you, I will come again and will take you to myself, so that where I am, there you may be also." Consequently, we Christians expect to dwell in heaven with Jesus, where together, we will live happily ever after.

I wonder if Jesus dwelling with us in heaven represents the whole picture of the next life. Obviously, Jesus will be in heaven. But it seems highly questionable to me that Jesus would be content to spend all of his time in heaven with proper folks while he ignores those who suffer in hell. When Jesus lived among us, he spent a high percentage of his time with outcasts, tax collectors, and sinners. In fact, he spent so much time with them, was so accepting of them and so open in his association with them that his actions seemed scandalous to the proper religious folks of his day.

The Scriptures tell us; "Now all the tax collectors and sinners were coming near to listen to him. And the Pharisees and the scribes were grumbling and saying, 'This fellow welcomes sinners and eats with them'" (Luke 15:1-2). "When the scribes of the Pharisees saw that he was eating with sinners and tax collectors, they said to his disciples, 'Why does he eat with tax collectors and sinners?' When Jesus heard this, he said to them, 'Those who are well have no need of a physician, but those who are sick; I have come to call not the righteous but sinners'" (Mark 2:16-17).

In light of how Jesus lived, and what his priorities were when he walked among us, I believe it is totally logical to conclude that Jesus would not spend all of his time exclusively with people enjoying heaven while ignoring those who suffer in hell. Since "Jesus Christ is the same yesterday and today and forever" (Hebrews 13: 8), I believe that, as long as there are people in hell, Jesus will spend much time with them, offering them support, encouragement, healing, forgiveness, and wholeness. Of course, since Jesus is Spirit, he is not limited to ministering in one place at a time, but can exercise his love and power in both heaven and hell simultaneously.

We affirm that Jesus saves people from hell each time we recite the Apostles' Creed. The traditional version reads that Jesus was "crucified, dead and buried; He descended into hell." Why did Jesus descend into hell? It's been taught ever since the time of the early Church that Jesus descended into hell to preach the good news to the lost, to rescue them.

We have already noted in Chapter One that Philippians 2:10-11 and 1 Peter 3:18-20; 4:6 make specific reference to Jesus saving people from hell. I believe Jesus will never rest as long as anyone remains in hell. I am confident that countless Christians will join with Jesus, their leader, in a great mission to rescue those who suffer. And they will not quit, either, until the last person is liberated from hell.

The concept of Jesus rescuing people from hell is consistent with what Dr. Maurice Rawlings learned from people he had resuscitated after they had been considered clinically dead. Some of those people who had near-death experiences reported having experienced hell. Several of them told of being saved from hell by Jesus or by the power of God. One person wrote regarding hell:

> There is no way to escape, no way out. You don't even try to look for one. This is the prison out of which no one can escape except by Divine intervention. . . . I saw another man coming by in front of us. I knew immediately who He was. He had a strong, kind, compassionate face, composed and unafraid, Master of all He saw. It was Jesus Himself.
>
> A great hope took hold of me and I knew the answer to my problem was this great and wonderful Person. . . . I did not do anything to attract His attention. I said again to myself, 'If He would only look my way and see me, He could rescue me from this place because He would know what to do.' He passed on by and it seemed as though He would not look my way, but just before He passed out of sight He turned His head and looked directly at me. That is all it took. His look was enough.[4]

Chapter Three

AMAZING GRACE

Implications Of Universal Salvation
Versus Eternal Damnation

The most basic and profound of all issues pertaining to the Christian faith is whether God will eventually save everyone. Contemplation of this issue brings forth many questions, such as: Is God our advocate or our adversary? If God were against us, wouldn't we need someone to save us from God? On the other hand, if God is for us, who can prevent God from saving us all?

As you can see, the very integrity of God is at stake with the issue of whether or not God will eventually save everyone. We might wonder, is God really all loving, and merciful and gracious? Or, is God a highly judgmental God who holds a grudge for eternity against those who are either not good enough to deserve to go to heaven, or who did not receive salvation before they died?

God is More Gracious than Humans
It is commonly accepted that God is gracious, loving and merciful. In spite of what the Bible says in support of God's gracious loving mercy, however, much of what passes as religion denies the existence of such a God. God is instead

often understood as a moral force in the universe that rewards the good and punishes those who are evil. But if God's only function is to be a supernatural bookkeeper, recording everyone's behavior and rewarding or punishing accordingly, then where is God's grace?

People who reject the idea of a God of eternal damnation sometimes tell me that if it was their decision, they would have mercy on people suffering in hell, and they would forgive the sufferers when they repented and allow them into heaven. Then they go further, to say something like, "If God is less loving, merciful and forgiving than I am, and if God's thirst for vengeance is so insatiable that an eternity of torment will not satisfy it, I don't want to have anything to do with God." (And I cannot blame them.) A God of that nature is certainly not appealing or attractive, and would clearly seem to be of a much different nature than God as presented by Jesus, whom he called "Father" ["Abba," (Mark 14:36), which could appropriately be translated, "Daddy"].

While talking with people who believe in an everlasting punishment in hell, I have often asked the question, "If you were God, would you consign some people to hell and then abandon them forever?" Not one of those people has been willing to answer that question. Without exception, they have either refused to answer it all together or they have tried to avoid it by saying something like, "I'm not God, so it's not a valid question," or "It doesn't matter what I would do." They seem to realize very quickly that if they say they would abandon people in hell, it would make them seem very uncaring and hard-hearted. Of course, they do not perceive themselves in that way. They realize that if they were really honest with themselves they would have to answer, "No". They are smart enough to realize it presents a serious problem for them to say they would not abandon people in hell, while they contend that God would do so. That would mean they believe God is less compassionate than they are. Because they do not want to seem so foolish as to suggest God is morally and ethically inferior to them, they choose to avoid answering the original question.

As for myself, as imperfect as I am, I would never consider abandoning even one person to endless hell. It is hard for me to imagine that anyone else would do so either. Perhaps some of us would be inclined to abandon certain individuals for a while, but not forever. I absolutely cannot believe God is morally or ethically inferior to me or other humans, so I cannot believe God would abandon anyone in hell.

God is More Gracious than Parents

If any of us continually and severely punished a child of our own for the rest of his life rather than listening to and acting on his pleas for mercy, we would either be put in jail or a mental hospital. Abuse happens all too often. People who are guilty of such offenses are locked up. How can we believe God would do something for which we mortals would be judged criminal or insane?

Sometimes a severely strained relationship develops between a child and his parents. Usually things can be worked out in a positive way, but occasionally the situation escalates to the extent that the parents, through an expression of "tough love," expel the child from their home. Even in an extreme situation this effort is not meant as a permanent expulsion. If a child truly changes and starts doing what is right, the parents normally welcome the child back into a new and positive relationship.

Surely there are parents in heaven whose children have very deservedly found themselves expelled from the fullness of life to suffer in hell. It is hard to imagine parents so hard-hearted as to deny the possibility of their children's transformation and release from hell, no matter how much difficulty their children might have given them. In fact, anybody worthy of dwelling in heaven will desire release from hell, not only for their own children, but also for their friends, neighbors, and even their enemies. Especially their enemies! According to Matthew 5:43-47, Jesus says,

⁴³"You have heard that it was said, 'You shall love

your neighbor and hate your enemy.' [44]But I say to you, Love your enemies and pray for those who persecute you, [45]so that you may be children of your Father in heaven; for he makes his sun rise on the evil and on the good, and sends rain on the righteous and on the unrighteous. [46]For if you love those who love you, what reward do you have? Do not even the tax collectors do the same? [47]And if you greet only your brothers and sisters, what more are you doing than others? Do not even the Gentiles do the same?'"

This passage makes it clear that loving one's enemies is what distinguishes Christians from non-Christians. Surely God steadfastly remains at least as loving, forgiving and accepting as any parent or any Christian in this life or the next.

The parent/child relationship, into which God calls us, is based on love not fear. Unfortunately, some preachers and well-meaning zealots attempt to scare people into heaven by saying things such as, "Be good or you will be punished," or "Accept Jesus as your Savior or God will send you to hell forever." Whether these thoughts are spoken boldly aloud or passed along by innuendo, the well-meaning messengers will attempt to justify using such scare tactics because they believe it is extremely important for people to be saved before it is too late. They also believe their tactics are the most effective means to accomplish their goal. According to them, the end justifies the means. Sadly, they often do not accomplish the desired results. Instead, the experiences that result are often the very stumbling blocks that cause yearning souls to become wary.

Surely we can all realize that no wise and loving father would seek to win his children through fear. The same is true of God. God does not want us to be afraid of God. Obviously, it is appropriate for us to have reverence for God and to approach God with awe in our hearts. In that sense, it is right to "fear" God, and to fear sinning because with our sin we wound God, ourselves, those who are close to us, and others in an ever-increasing circle. God calls us into a relationship of love, not fear. Fear denies and prevents the welcoming and loving nature of the relationship into which God calls us.

Gracious but Not Soft on Sin

Our affirmation of universal salvation does not mean we would suggest God is soft on sin. We all know sin is a terribly tragic thing. It causes people to experience hell. God will not pat everyone on the head and say, "There, there, I'm sure you didn't mean it. It's all right. Go on in to heaven and enjoy yourself." Sin is very serious. It is so serious that God sent his Son to save us from it. It is so serious that Jesus was willing to die to overcome it. Because sin is so serious, we should be eternally grateful God did not give up on us, but instead came to our rescue.

Declaring it is possible for a person to make the transition from hell to heaven does not deny the reality or the significance of hell. It does not minimize the seriousness of sin or the severity of one's misery while in hell either, both of which are well documented in the Bible. It does, however, allow us to know God to be the kind of God Jesus personified and described, having infinite love, power, mercy and grace.

Many Lack Opportunities to be Saved

Often people do not have a reasonable opportunity to experience salvation before they die. Many grow up in homes where there is no interest in the Church, or where there is outright hostility toward anything Christian. Some people suffer harsh experiences with the Church and, as a result, do not want to associate with Christians, often because of Christians' hypocrisy, where their actions are inconsistent with what they profess to believe. Others, as children, endure a bad relationship with their father and consequently, cannot bring themselves to love and serve a God whom people call "Father". Some people are led astray by cults and subjected to brainwashing. Still others go through life without hearing sufficiently of God's salvation.

So there are many, many valid reasons why people may not

experience a fair opportunity to be saved before they die. If we think about it, we might ask, "What is to become of all of those people?" Surely God would not be so unreasonable and unfair as to consign them to suffer in hell forever on the technicality that they had not accepted salvation before their death!

By the same token, how about those who did apparently have many good opportunities to accept salvation during their lifetime, and for whatever reasons failed to do so? Is it fair or right that they be consigned to hell forever with no further opportunity for conversion? Even with many opportunities, who is to say that they received an adequate amount of exposure to the faith to result in conversion? In many cases, perhaps one more chance was all it might have taken for them to have accepted their salvation. Would God be so unreasonable as to deny them that one saving opportunity? Surely not!

There are religions other than Christianity. Is it possible to be saved through them? The billions of people around the world who have grown up under the influence of other religions again may not have had a fair chance to hear and respond favorably to the Christian gospel. Obviously, if they are saved through other religions, billions of people (non-Christians) will enter into heaven following death. But if they are not saved, they will all suffer in hell. If that is the case, could God be so uncaring as to forever deny release from hell even for those who faithfully followed their religious convictions in this life?

Trying to Get God Off the Hook

If God consigns sinners to hell to suffer forever without any opportunity to make amends wouldn't that very idea suggest God is something of a monster? Those who believe in eternal damnation but are not willing to concede that God is a monster often seek to find ways to get God off the hook. Some even go to the extreme of maintaining that endless hell is a manifestation of God's love. Perhaps the most well known attempt to do this was by Dante in *The Inferno*.

The Inferno is Dante's perception of hell. In his writing, incorrigible sinners were so tortured because of their own evil it was not deemed necessary or appropriate for external punishment to be imposed upon them, the way hell is usually perceived. Justice allowed sinners to suffer only from what they brought on themselves due to their sinful condition, and no more. However, if they were exposed to the holy light of God's unveiled presence they suffered more greatly. Therefore, according to Dante's view, because God continued to love everyone, even those who had rebelled against God, God provided hell as a refuge from God's presence. It was not out of wrath or vengeance that God created hell, but it was done as a result of God's unending love for all people. According to this way of thinking, "God could not remove the inherent pain of evil being, but he could and did provide a refuge from a greater pain. And so justice and love built hell, the painful refuge."[1]

Even though this explanation is seemingly well intentioned, I believe it is a very inadequate attempt to get God off the hook. It amounts to a rationalization those believers of eternal damnation use to prove that God is not a monster even though God is perceived by them to do monstrous things. Wouldn't it be better for all of us to give up the monstrous misunderstanding about God and eternal damnation in hell so it would be no longer necessary for us to rationalize?

Christ's Victory Is Complete

Interestingly, I have found some variations in the beliefs held among theologians and Church leaders who espouse universal salvation. As an example, some teach that hell is experienced only in this life. They declare that Christ has provided salvation for everyone, whether they realize it and accept it or not. Thus, they teach that there will be no hell after death and everyone will go to heaven because of Christ's victory.

I agree that Christ's victory is universal and complete. But, I cannot accept the non-existence of hell after death. The Bible teaches us about hell in the next life as well as in this life. Many people are still rejecting God at the time of their death, so they are presumably destined for hell unless they are to become converted immediately following death. I believe this probably happens with many people, though I am not aware of any biblical teaching that suggests this will be the case with everyone. Consequently, I must conclude that even though salvation through Christ is complete, some people, while not realizing they are saved, will continue to live as though they are lost and thus, experience hell until they are converted.

Renowned twentieth century Swiss theologian, Karl Barth, says that people who are not saved isolate themselves from God by resisting the salvation that has already been provided through Christ. God is for them but they are against God. God receives them but they withdraw from God. God is gracious to them but they are ungrateful to God. God forgives their sins but they repeat them as though they are not forgiven.[2] I believe God will eventually help everyone realize and accept that Christ has already provided salvation for them, and lead them to heaven, including, when necessary, to save people from hell.

A Joyous Affirmation

After years of careful research and prayerful contemplation of all the information that I have presented to you, I feel joyfully compelled to affirm that God will eventually save everyone. Since I have begun openly revealing my belief, I have discovered that many others have reached the same conclusion (though they are often reluctant to express it). In this conclusion, I am in complete agreement with Leslie Weatherhead, where in his book, *Life Begins at Death*, he writes,

> My own view is that God wills that every living soul shall at last be brought by free choice into harmony with His will. I understand that it may be aeons of time, as we think of time, before everyone is brought in. But the Bible seems to be very strong on this point

that all shall be saved and come to a knowledge of the truth. So I believe that finally, without any coercion or any unfair use of force, the soul will come to see that its highest welfare is in saying "Yes" to God. And that finally this will happen and all created beings will be brought into harmony with God, in an ultimate heaven the nature of which we simply haven't the power to imagine.[3]

Chapter Four

I WANT TO DO IT MYSELF

Do We Have Free Will?

We all like to believe we are in charge of our lives, that we can take care of ourselves. We have been taught to be self-sufficient and to not accept charity because to do so reflects weakness and dishonor. This way of thinking has become so deeply ingrained in some of us that we might even feel uneasy about accepting a gift offered us by a friend. Our self-sufficiency also carries over into our religious beliefs where it causes us to conclude that, of our own free will, we are able to do whatever is necessary to save ourselves.

Ephesians 2:8-9 says, "For by grace you have been saved through faith, and this is not of your own doing; it is the gift of God - not the result of works, so that no one may boast." Even though this passage makes it clear that we are saved by grace instead of good works, many of us still find great difficulty in accepting that free gift. We want very much to earn our salvation.

Some people put much emphasis on free will. Obviously, we do have freedom. We make choices every day. But are we totally free? That is the question we must address as we deal with the issues of how we are saved and whether anyone might spend eternity in hell.

God Will Prevail

I get the impression that some people are not particularly bothered by the prospect that certain other people might be consigned to hell forever. They explain, "As I see it, some people choose to be saved so they can get in to heaven. Others choose to reject God. Because of that, they should go to hell. It's too bad, but it's a choice they made of their own free will." It is as if they are saying, "I had the good sense to get myself saved, and if other people aren't as wise as me, well, too bad."

It makes me ask, are some people saved only because they use good sense? Does this also mean others go to hell because they freely make bad choices? I believe the only reason we are able to choose salvation is because of our being drawn to God by God's grace and power. And the only reason we might reject God is because we are frightened, misguided people. Because some people continue to reject God, they go to hell after they die. But I believe God does not simply give up on them. So, while we do have free will to a degree, we do not possess it to the extent that we can resist God forever. It is not logical, nor is there anything in the Bible that might lead us to believe that any human would be able to resist forever the advances, the wooing of Almighty God, the creator. Is the creature ever more powerful than the creator?

Do we have total free will? Are we completely free to make choices that result in either happiness or misery? Obviously, we sometimes do things that cause us pain. Are these totally free choices or are they the result of influences (such as alcoholism, drug addiction or difficult family situations) that are often beyond our control? If we have complete free will to make choices, as some people suggest, wouldn't it be illogical for us to choose to live in a way that would cause us to experience hell? And if we continue to have freedom of choice in the next life, wouldn't it be utterly absurd to choose to continue to suffer in hell forever? The alternative would be to accept the joy, peace, and forgiveness (the eternal life) that God by grace continually offers. Choosing eternal life is an easy choice, it seems to me. That is, if we really do have complete free will.

On the other hand, what if people do not have total freedom? What if there are negative influences that compel us to sometimes go astray or make bad choices? If that is the case, would God condemn misguided people to hell forever, or would God overcome those negative forces and save everyone? Both the Bible and logic tell us, yes; God would do so.

Salvation for the Worst of Sinners

Some people are sympathetic to the teaching of universal salvation, and want to affirm it. But they find difficulty with the idea that notorious sinners or criminals could ever be saved. Short of denying free will all together for those wretched sinners who have the propensity to repeatedly make bad choices, some people cannot imagine those unfortunate souls ever being saved.

The important truth we need to keep in mind here is that no one is more powerful than God. No one can resist God's grace forever. We are like children trying to dam up a rushing mountain stream before it can water the valley below. We may be successful for a while, but the waters keep rising against the rocks. Inevitably, the water surges over the dam and tumbles down to the valley where it quenches the thirst of all who wait for it. Surely we can see that when God combines a steady stream of love and grace with as much time as this process takes to convert each person, God will prevail in any quest to save even the most hardened sinner.

Happily, we are all destined for salvation. That which is destined is something over which we have no choice and which we cannot prevent. By definition, our destiny is in God's hands and is predetermined by God. Whether we like it or not, or believe it or not, or even work with all our might against it, we cannot stop God from saving everyone.

God Is Not a Monster

Does God allow some people to condemn themselves forever of their own free will? Noted contemporary author,

Robert Short, states in his book, *Something To Believe In*, that if that is the case it would make God one kind of monster or another. "He is either the weak God of unlimited love but limited power, or else he is the cruel God of unlimited power but limited love."[1]

The weak God who possesses unlimited love but limited power would choose to limit God's own power in order to give people free will, supposedly out of love. Such a God could then only helplessly stand by as God's children freely damn themselves. Wouldn't that be like the father who told his young child to stay in the yard and then did nothing more while his child walked onto the street to be killed when he was struck by a passing car? Surely any loving earthly father would do everything he could to prevent harm from coming to his child. Certainly God would do the same. We make God to be a monster if we believe God would not use God's great power to save all of us, but would instead say something like, "It's his own fault. He knew what he was doing. It's just too bad he disobeyed me."

With the second kind of monster, God possesses unlimited power but limited love. This kind of God resembles an eight hundred pound gorilla that can do whatever he wants. No one can stop him. Here there is no pretense that people have been given free will. God is totally in charge, although not necessarily being guided or restrained by love. God, according to this way of thinking, consigns most people to eternal damnation without any regret, and saves only a chosen few.

The teaching of eternal damnation makes it impossible to believe that God is both all loving and all-powerful, but necessitates that God be one or the other type of monster Gods. Neither of these two images of God is particularly appealing, or supported by Scripture.

Martin Luther on Free Will

Martin Luther, who began the Protestant Reformation in 1517, celebrated the fact that he did not have total free will, but instead was saved by God's grace and mercy. He states; "I frankly confess that, for myself, even if it could be, I should not want "free-will" to be given me. . . . But now that God has taken my salvation out of the control of my own will, and put it under the control of His, and promised to save me, not according to my working or running, but according to His own grace and mercy, I have the comfortable certainty that He is faithful and will not lie to me, and that He is also great and powerful, so that no devils or opposition can break Him or pluck me from Him."[2]

The Idolatry of Free Will

It is of great significance that when Jesus was on the cross, he did not pray, saying, "Father, throw them all into hell because they have free will and they know very well what they are doing." Instead, he said, "Father, forgive them; for they do not know what they are doing" (Luke 23:34). This Scripture suggests we don't have total free will, but it makes it clear we are forgiven. What power there is in unconditional love and forgiveness! We will be exploring those concepts at length in chapter seven.

Believing that we are saved by free will denies Scripture. According to the book of John, Jesus says, "No one can come to me unless drawn by the Father who sent me" (John 6:44); "Apart from me you can do nothing" (John 15:5); and "You did not choose me but I chose you" (John 15:6).

Most importantly, the doctrine of free will denies God and results in idolatry, of worshipping and trusting oneself instead of God. Not completely trusting in God, people tend to resist placing the all-important matter of whether they end up in heaven or hell entirely in God's hands. This position can be expressed in Robert Short's words, as follows: "Please step aside, God. In this little matter of where we're going to spend eternity, we'll decide ourselves with our own 'free wills', thank you!"[3] May we all avoid this kind of idolatry.

Karl Barth took a very dim view of save-yourself religion. For Barth, the term "religion" had the negative connotation of do-it-yourself salvation. Barth believed Christianity was the only true religion, and the proper understanding of Christianity was that people could not do anything to save themselves. He emphasized that only God saves, and people are not God. Robert Short also says, "All do-it-yourself salvation schemes are actually either unconscious or disguised atheism."[4] Ultimately, do-it-yourself-ers trust in themselves rather than in God for their salvation.

The Irresistible God

If we are not saved because of making good decisions by our free will, but God saves us by acting irresistibly, does that mean we have lost our freedom? John Wesley, the founder of the Methodist movement in the eighteenth century, said that is not the case. In fact, he claimed that everyone in the world could be saved without the loss of liberty, according to a sermon entitled, "The General Spread of The Gospel," which he preached on April 22, 1783. He said that a city, nation, or the whole world could become Christian, and that it could take place without difficulty if only we suppose that God acts irresistibly. It would be as when God created the world. God said, "Let there be light" (Genesis 1:3) and there was light.

Wesley then went on to tell the listeners that, when they were converted, God did not take away their understanding but it was enlightened and strengthened; God did not destroy their affections but they were made more vigorous than before; God did not take away their liberty, their power of choosing between good and evil; God did not force them but because of being assisted by God's grace they chose the better way. "Now in the same manner as God *has* converted so many to himself without destroying their liberty, he *can* undoubtedly convert whole nations, or the whole world. And it is as easy to him to convert a world as one individual soul."[5]

Some people speak of human freedom as if it is the highest of all values. They are even willing to consign countless people to endless hell in order to maintain the doctrine of free will. But, in the end, I believe there is a higher standard involved here than whether or not people have total free will or liberty.

Isn't it more important that people be saved than that their freedom be left totally intact? We have already established that God can save the whole world without violating our free will. But even if that were not the case, surely a loving God would interfere with human freedom in certain ways if it were necessary in order to prevent anyone from becoming eternally lost.

There are at least two situations in which humans would feel justified in interfering with the freedom of others. We, first of all, would feel justified in preventing one person from doing harm to another. Because of this, a loving father might report his own son to the police in an effort to prevent him from committing a crime. We would also feel justified in preventing others from doing great harm to themselves. So a parent might even physically restrain his or her child in an effort to prevent him from injuring himself. Just as loving parents would restrict the freedom of their children, so too we can be sure that if it were necessary, God would restrict the freedom of the children God loves in order to save them.

So the reality of the situation is that we humans have free will, and we use it to make many decisions every day. But we do not have total freedom when it comes to the issue of where we will spend eternity. A loving God could never have created a world in which we, through our free will, would have the capacity to damn ourselves for eternity. Instead, even in our freedom, God guides us all into union with Godself. Thanks be to God!

Chapter Five

LAYING A SOLID FOUNDATION

What God Is Like

What we believe about God is the foundation of our faith. The rest of our religious beliefs are built upon those underpinnings. If our understanding of God is naive, antiquated or reflects only part of what the Bible says, then our other religious beliefs will inevitably be misguided. But if our perception of God is more nearly complete and enlightened, then the rest of what we believe will be enlightened also. Certainly our understanding of God is central to our discussion about universal salvation versus eternal damnation.

Before we get into this, I believe it is important for us to acknowledge that it is impossible to fully understand the nature of God. It would be very naive of anyone to think that he or she knew all there was to know about God. But it is important to do our best to understand as much as we can regarding what God is like.

In this chapter, I would like for us to look beyond some very important matters, such as: God's mercy, grace, patience, forgiveness, power, and desire to save everyone. Volumes could be written about each of those topics, and have been. For the purposes of this book, I believe I've dealt with those matters at sufficient length in other chapters. It is important now that I say more about God in a general sense.

In our quest to try to determine what God is like we need to consider God from several perspectives, such as: Is God the God of only select people, or the God of everyone? What does God as Spirit mean? What is the divine nature? What did Jesus mean when he said, "The kingdom of God is within you." (Luke 17:21)?

To help us in our understanding of God, I'd like to begin with early Old Testament thinking and follow the progression of thought into the New Testament, especially focusing on the words of Jesus. In doing this, we should not assume that the Old Testament was written in strict chronological order from beginning to end. More importantly, it's helpful to realize it was common for writers (sometimes hundreds of years later) to make revisions or additions to the earlier books. Those writers felt free to make changes and additions because they did not come to consider those books to be Scripture until hundreds of years after they were originally written. Consequently, some books are a blend of very early writings interspersed with material added much later. So, while following the progression of thinking of the people in ancient times, one cannot always rely on where particular passages appear in the Old Testament to indicate chronology. Another complication is that, as in our day, people of historical times did not all agree; so different concepts often existed side by side over long periods of time. As I follow the teachings through the Old Testament, I will not attempt to indicate precisely when given passages were written. Instead, with very broad strokes, I will seek to present a general chronological progression of thought.

Family Deity

In very early Old Testament times, each family or tribe believed they had their own god. So, according to Exodus 3:1-5, when God appeared to Moses in a burning bush to call him to lead the Israelites out of their slavery in Egypt and on to the Promised Land, Moses asked God to identify himself. He needed to determine which god he was speaking to from among the many gods that were perceived to exist in that day.

He knew he would have to tell the Israelites who had sent him. God replied, "Thus you shall say to the Israelites, 'The LORD, the God of your ancestors, the God of Abraham, the God of Isaac, and the God of Jacob, has sent me to you'" (Exodus 3:15). As we can see, God was initially perceived to be a very exclusive god, relating only to one family or tribe.

Wizard of Oz

As the centuries passed the prophets helped to expand people's perception of God. For example, Isaiah writes, "I am the LORD, and there is no other; besides me there is no god. . . . All of them are put to shame and confounded, the makers of idols go in confusion together. But Israel is saved by the LORD with everlasting salvation" (Isaiah 45:5,16-17). With the help of the prophets people came to realize there is only one God, the God who created the universe and who is the God of all nations. They generally thought of God as being up there or out there; the Supreme Being who lives somewhere out beyond the world; the God who set everything in motion, and periodically intervenes in the running of the world or in people's lives; the God who they expected to send a Messiah to earth like a visitor from above to provide salvation for humankind.

This is what I would call the Wizard of Oz perception of God. According to this understanding, God is perhaps a kindly old gentleman with gray hair and a long beard, who sits up in heaven with all of his knowledge and wisdom, and pulls strings to dramatically demonstrate his awesome power.

Spirit

Well before the end of Old Testament times and the birth of Jesus, the Israelites began to move beyond the Wizard of Oz understanding of God. This was done for practical reasons. They wondered, for example, if God resided in heaven, how could God hear and answer prayers from everyone all over the world at the same time? There had to be a better way to perceive what God is like.

Picture, if you will, a giant switchboard with perhaps

hundreds or thousands of operators taking the calls from people and putting them on hold so that God can answer the calls in the order they are received. With that system, it could take a long time to get your prayers answered, and then it might happen only if you did not get cut off by some mistake.

Because they gave thought to the true nature of God, the Israelites began to realize that God is spirit, that God is not confined to the body of a kindly old gentleman in heaven, but could be everywhere and relate with everyone at the same time. Hebrew, the language of the ancient Israelites, helped them to comprehend what God as spirit means. The Hebrew word *ruach* relates three meanings; wind, breath and spirit. The Israelites came to understand that God's spirit was like the air we breathe or like the blowing of the wind. They realized that, like the air or wind, God was not visible, yet was the source of life and that you could be aware of God's power when God acts.

Consider the creation story: "The earth was a formless void and darkness covered the face of the deep, while a wind from God swept over the face of the waters" (Genesis 1:2). and "Then the LORD God formed man from the dirt of the ground, and breathed into his nostrils the breath of life; and the man became a living being" (Genesis 2:7).

In building on this theme Jesus said, "The wind blows where it chooses, and you hear the sound of it, but you do not know where it comes from or where it goes. So it is with everyone who is born of the Spirit" (John 3:8). Jesus further said, "God is spirit, and those who worship him must worship in spirit and truth" (John 4:24); and "Where two or three are gathered in my name, I am there among them" (Matthew 18:20). After Jesus rose from the dead, he met with his disciples and "he breathed on them and said to them, 'Receive the Holy Spirit'" (John 20:22).

Higher Power

As a way of understanding God as spirit, in the Alcoholics Anonymous program people refer to God as a Higher Power.

When I first heard that expression I responded negatively. "Why don't you just call God, God?" I thought, "Why use the term Higher Power?"

Of course, one explanation is that the expression, Higher Power is a generic term, and it is generally not offensive. That is especially beneficial to the alcoholics who may have had religion forced on them as young people. As a result, they have turned against religion, and the term God is not something they are comfortable with either. So they use the less threatening term, Higher Power. Nobody is offended, and they often can quickly begin to relate very well to their Higher Power. It is also very helpful to use the term Higher Power for those who have never been introduced to religion at all, and for people who believe in many guiding forces rather than one God.

Related to initially questioning the use of the term Higher Power, I also thought it would be good for the people in the Alcoholics Anonymous program to eventually graduate to a more advanced way of thinking. In my perception of this, they would no longer use the term Higher Power, but would just refer to God as God. I have since realized the error of my ways. I have decided that perhaps some of the rest of us are the ones who need to graduate. Our common understanding of the term God tends to put God in a box, which greatly limits our perception of God. For some, the term God conjures up images of a kindly old gentleman who sits in heaven, pulling strings, causing it to lightening and thunder, etc. On the other hand, the term Higher Power tends to not be so limiting of God. It comes closer to allowing God to be what God is. That is, a loving spiritual being who is present with each one of us.

The Higher Power is understood in many different ways. The alcoholic may understand the Higher Power as a spiritual and personal force that helps people remain sober. For some members of Alcoholics Anonymous, the AA group itself is that Higher Power or the source of the Higher Power, since the power to stay sober comes from their fellow members. I was once told of a man who considered his lawn mower to be his Higher Power. This man spent a lot of time mowing the lawn.

Staying busy with his mower kept him from drinking. When the mower broke down he would spend hours trying to fix it. It seemed like the mower resisted fixing; that the mower was smarter than he was. He believed the mower's successful resistance to getting fixed was its way of keeping him from drinking. He spent much of his time working on the mower, which in turn prevented him from getting together with his drinking buddies. So his lawn mower was his Higher Power. (I wonder if his snow blower became his Higher Power in the wintertime.)

One day the man had an accident with the mower, which resulted in the loss of a toe. His Higher Power had cut off his toe, he thought, just because he had made a mistake. What a deal! What an angry Higher Power! Not surprisingly, the man changed his Higher Power to something more forgiving of his mistakes after that.

Unfortunately, it seems many people have that kind of understanding of God. Toe the line or he will cut off your toe, or something worse. There is a better way to perceive God; that is, to realize God is on our side, would never harm us, wants the best for us and will ultimately make that a reality.

Thinking of God as spirit is very helpful in understanding how God can be with each of us at the same time. That is certainly something we can affirm and celebrate. God is not just the Almighty who created the universe but is as close to us as the air we breathe and loves us more than we can even comprehend. God sent Jesus to be our Savior, so we can have fullness of life now and go to be with God forever after we die.

Oneness with Humankind

It would be great to stop right here in our understanding of God. But the Bible compels us to go on to an even deeper perception and appreciation. What we have established so far is that God as the Creator is as far away as the most distant galaxy. At the same time, God is very close to us and we can even appropriately think of God as coming into us as the air we breathe and also as living in our hearts. But with this perception, God is still considered a different kind of being from humans, and one who is completely separate from humans. There are some passages of Scripture, however, which indicate that God is not completely different or separate from us.

Jesus, when he walked among us as a human, was not totally different or separate from God. He said, "The Father and I are one" (John 10:30), and "The Father is in me and I am in the Father" (John 10:38). Jesus experienced a oneness with God. If Jesus as a human enjoyed that kind of relationship with God, why would it not also be true of the rest of us? Many will say Jesus was different because he was not only human but divine as well. There are indications Jesus did not see it that way.

Psalms 82:6 reads, "I say, 'You are gods, children of the Most High, all of you.'" It is of great significance that Jesus quoted this Psalm in the midst of an encounter with some of the Jewish leaders. After Jesus said, "The Father and I are one" (John 10:30), some of the people threatened to kill him by stoning. They told him it was "For blasphemy, because you, though only a human being, are making yourself God." Jesus answered, "Is it not written in your law, 'I said, you are gods?' If those to whom the word of God came were called 'gods' - and the scripture cannot be annulled - can you say that the one whom the Father has sanctified and sent into the world is blaspheming because I said, 'I am God's Son'?" (John 10:33-36).

So Jesus claims to be divine. And the argument he uses to support that claim is that since other people are referred to as gods, they should not think it is inappropriate that Jesus claims to be God's Son. In this case then, Jesus, in considering himself to be one with God or to be divine, did not perceive that he was different from others. Along this same line, 2 Peter 1:3,4 reads, "His divine power has given us everything needed for life and godliness. . .Thus, he has given us. . .his precious and very great promises, so that through him you. . .may become participants of the divine nature."

Beyond this, Jesus told his followers, "The kingdom of God is within you" (Luke 17:21). Also, according to John 17:20-21, Jesus said in prayer for his followers, "I ask not only on behalf of these, but also on behalf of those who will believe in me through their word, that they may all be one. As you, Father, are in me and I am in you, may they also be in us."

Jesus' disciple Philip asked Jesus to show them the Father. Jesus replied, "Whoever has seen me has seen the Father. How can you say, 'Show us the Father?' Do you not believe that I am in the Father and the Father is in me? The words that I say to you I do not speak on my own; but the Father who dwells in me does his works" (John 14:9-10). Jesus then goes on to say something which I believe is astonishing; "Very truly, I tell you, the one who believes in me will also do the works that I do and, in fact, will do greater works than these" (John 14:12).

Jesus does claim to be one with God, but he also says that the same is true of us. He claims to do great work because God is in him and he declares that we by God's power will do even greater works. So Jesus does not set himself apart from other humans, and he encourages us to affirm our oneness with God and to live powerfully and victoriously in that relationship. C. S. Lewis, twentieth century British teacher and prolific author, affirms this high understanding and expectation of humankind. He writes,

> Now the whole offer which Christianity makes is this: that we can, if we let God have His way, come to share in the life of Christ. If we do, we shall then be sharing a life which was begotten, not made, which always has existed and always will exist. Christ is the Son of God. If we share in this kind of life we also shall be sons of God. We shall love the Father as He does and the Holy Ghost will arise in us. He came to this world and became a man in order to spread to other men the kind of life He has--by what I call "good infection." Every Christian is to become a little Christ. The whole purpose of becoming a Christian is simply nothing else.[1]

Ground of Our Being

Now we need to go back to our discussion of what God is like and ask again, is God totally different and separate from humans? It seems to me we have to answer, "no". But if God is not completely different and separate from us, what are we to make of that? How do we understand it?

We need to begin by taking a look at the concepts of immanence and transcendence. To speak of the immanence of God is to refer to the closeness of God to us, the indwelling divinity within human beings, God being in us and us being in God, and being one with God. I will be saying much more about that. But to keep things in balance I need to first say some things about transcendence. The transcendence of God refers to the divinity that is external to us humans, and is creator, one who is all-powerful, all knowing and everywhere present, including in heaven. A combined understanding of God as immanent and transcendent is essential. If we focus on one at the exclusion of the other, we limit or distort our understanding of God.

Paul Tillich, the twentieth century German-born U.S. theologian, helped us make sense of this when he said God is "the creative ground of everything that has being, that, in fact, he is the infinite and unconditional power of being or, in the most radical abstraction, that he is being-itself. In this respect God is neither along side things nor even 'above' them; he is nearer to them than they are to themselves. He is their creative ground, here and now, always and everywhere."[2]

So God is the ground of our being, the source of our existence and much more. It means that God is in us and we are in God, and we are one with God. With this understanding of God, it is not completely satisfying or sufficient to say, "God is in his heaven: all is right with the world." God is out there but not only out there. If God were only out there, God could not be involved with the world or with us as individuals. When Tillich spoke of God he was not referring to a supernatural being beyond the world to whom we can turn, and whom we can depend upon to intervene from without.

Rather than being out there, in the Twentieth century German church leader and theologian, Dietrich Bonhoeffer's words, "God is beyond in the midst of our life."[3]

It is good to affirm that God is in us, but it is really more appropriate and accurate to put more emphasis on us being in God. That is because God is far too great and awesome to be fully contained in any one of us, or even in all of us. But we can all be fully contained in God. So while there is something of God in each of us, it is much better to speak of us as existing in God.

As I grew up, my parents and Sunday School teachers told me that God speaks to each of us through our conscience. That is one way to understand and affirm that God is in us. M. Scott Peck, author of *The Road Less Traveled*, associates the indwelling God with the unconscious part of our minds. He says, "The interface between God and man is at least in part the interface between our unconscious and our conscious."[4] I believe this explanation makes a lot of sense. It is consistent with God speaking to us through our conscience, and with the idea that the Holy Spirit resides in us. The unconscious part of our mind possesses extraordinary knowledge and wisdom.

The unconscious dimension of our minds is also the source of dreams, through which we can receive guidance from God. There are numerous references in the Bible to God speaking to people through their dreams, many of which are associated with the birth of Jesus. For example, Joseph considered breaking off his relationship with Mary after he learned she was pregnant with a child to be called Jesus. He assumed another man was the father. But "An angel of the Lord appeared to him in a dream and said, 'Joseph, son of David, do not be afraid to take Mary as your wife, for the child conceived in her is from the Holy Spirit'" (Matthew 1:20).

In Everything

There are several passages of Scripture that reflect the relationship between God and nature. Psalms 96:1,11-13 proclaims, "O sing to the Lord a new song; sing to the Lord, all the earth. Let the heavens be glad, and let the earth rejoice; let the sea roar, and all that fills it; let the field exalt, and everything in it. Then shall all the trees of the forest sing for joy before the Lord."

Some people have mistakenly gone to the extreme of concluding that God is synonymous with nature, that everything is God and God is everything. That belief is called pantheism. Pantheism is generally considered to be heresy because it robs God of transcendence. While it is important to affirm that God is in everything, it is essential to realize that God is also beyond everything.

This leads us to panentheism, not to be confused with the similarly spelled word pantheism. There is a profound difference between the two. Rather than the pantheistic view that everything is God and God is everything, panentheism means everything is in God and God is in everything. Matthew Fox says in his book, *Original Blessing,* "panentheism is a way of seeing the world sacramentally."[5] What this means is that we can experience God and be drawn closer to God through our contact with or exposure to all of God's creation. Panentheism helps us to celebrate the deep with-ness of God. The with-ness of God is referred to in the story of Jesus' birth, according to Matthew 1:23, as the angel of the Lord spoke to Joseph, saying "'Look, the virgin shall conceive and bear a son, and they shall name him Emmanuel,' which means, 'God is with us.'"

I'm aware that some people object to the idea that God is in everything. They claim that God is totally separate from creation, and contend that God is no more a part of creation than an artist is a part of his paintings. I disagree. In contrast to an artist, God is everywhere present. That being the case, how could God not be in everything?

Experienced Through Nature

The fact that God is not only in humans but is in all of creation explains why nature has such a strong appeal. I expect that many people do not consciously think of the enjoyment of nature as being a spiritual, God-encountering experience. I believe oftentimes it is primarily a deep unconscious (God inspired) hunger for the spiritual which compels people to engage in activities, such as; boating, fishing, hiking, bird-watching and star-gazing. Countless families go camping religiously every weekend during the summer. They may not even give a thought to what motivates them. I am convinced that if they looked deep into their souls they would realize that camping for them is a spiritual experience. They may even recognize how God is drawing them closer to God through the nature they love. Fishermen often will say, "It really doesn't matter if I catch any fish. It's just being out there that counts." Apparently they realize on some level that there is something much more important in their adventure than merely catching fish.

Those who go to the beach, especially to the ocean, typically have the same kinds of experiences. Personally, while I am close to the ocean or even better, in it, I feel that I am encountering the rhythm of life itself. It is to commune with God. I believe it is not an accident that those who go to the beach are called "sun worshippers." It is not that they are actually worshipping the sun, but just spending time on the beach provides them a worshipful, spiritual experience.

I can identify with those who are drawn to nature. Nature continually feeds my spirit. In fact, I have been enriched by some deeply moving spiritual, God-encountering experiences through nature that rival and perhaps even exceed any worship experiences I have enjoyed inside church buildings.

As a minister I register the usual concerns about the drop in attendance at worship during the summer. But I have been known on occasion to say that for certain individuals, rather than attending church every Sunday, they should go camping, fishing or visit the beach, instead. That is where they seem to have their deepest spiritual experiences. I would only hope, though, that they would recognize that it is God who leads them out into nature so they might be spiritually enriched.

The degree of spiritual enrichment through interaction with nature does not apply equally to everyone. Generally, people who feel guilty about their absence from church are being taught that church is where they are meant to be on a regular basis on Sunday mornings. It is in church where their spirits are most satisfactorily fed, more so than while they are out enjoying nature. They might better go to the woods after worship. But for those certain individuals, for whom the outdoors is their cathedral, they should contemplate nature on many Sundays.

I am not suggesting it is sufficient for anyone to experience God only through nature. The risk is that one might become merely a nature worshipper. To establish and maintain perspective, a person needs to become aware of Christian principles through activities such as Bible study, other reading, Sunday School and worship. Ideally, one should maintain a balance in spiritual disciplines. When a balanced perspective is maintained, experiencing nature can contribute significantly to spiritual growth and renewal.

With that understanding, people will be able to not only see their excursions as chances to get away from the routine of their lives, but as God-encountering opportunities as well. If they do, they will be perceptive to the spiritual experiences of life and will be moved to celebrate their many uplifting, life giving encounters with the Almighty, the Great Beyond in the midst of their lives. How wonderful it is that we can experience God through nature. It is an example of the many ways in which God reaches out to us and draws us to God for the purpose of eventually saving everyone.

Love

The ultimate understanding in regard to what God is like is to recognize that God is love. Some people not only affirm that God is love, but go to the extreme of contending that love is God. While I appreciate what they are saying and believe there is some validity to it, I cannot go that far myself. It seems to me that in saying that love is God one runs into pretty much the same difficulty as we do with pantheism, which means that God is everything and everything is God. In both cases, we limit what God can be. With pantheism we are saying God exists only as a part of the physical universe. In saying that love is God we limit God to existing only as love. So I would not go so far as to say that love is God. But we can and must conclude that God is love, and what a powerful affirmation that is.

We are told in John 3:16, "For God so loved the world that he gave his only Son, so that everyone who believes in him may not perish but may have eternal life." Also, 1 John 4:7-8, 16 states, "Beloved, let us love one another, because love is from God; everyone who loves is born of God and knows God. Whoever does not love does not know God, for God is love. . . Those who abide in love abide in God, and God abides in them."

To assert that God is love is to believe that when we experience love we are in touch with God. Matthew 18:20 reads, "Where two or three are gathered in my name, I am there among them." Not only does this mean that Jesus (or God) is present as an additional person, but is there and is experienced in the expressions of love between people.

More Thoughts About God

Now I would like to share some other important thoughts regarding what God is like. First of all, we must move beyond 1,000 B.C. in our understanding of God. Before that time, God was perceived to be a family, tribal or national deity. If we can go beyond that antiquated view of God we will be able to realize that no one possesses God. God is not just the God of Abraham, or the Israelites, or even Christians, but of everyone. No one has exclusive rights to God's grace. God's grace is not just for the benefit of Christians, for them alone to possess, but it is a universal gift God shares with the world.

The Bible makes it very clear that God is love. Any teaching that denies or minimizes that love runs contrary to the Bible. So, teaching that God locks people in hell and throws away the key has to be faulty. Claiming that God loves only the lovable or that God does not love those who are in hell must be seriously questioned. And saying God loves Billy Graham more than Adolf Hitler must be challenged. After all, who needs the transforming power of unconditional love more than Hitler? For God to withhold love from anyone would amount to admitting defeat. It is through the power of unconditional love that ultimate victory will be achieved. In chapter seven we will explore unconditional love in depth.

Since God is in us and we are in God and we are one with God, nothing can separate us from God. For God to abandon anyone in hell would amount to God abandoning Godself. That is impossible for God to do. God is not just a detached, high and mighty being who pronounces judgments on people from a distance. Instead, God is the ground of our being, the meaning of our existence, far away and intimately close, powerful and gentle, saving and loving. God is not hostile but friendly.

Over the centuries the Church has largely lost its appreciation of the fact that the Scriptures say God is in us and we are in God, we are one with God and we are participants of the divine nature. According to L. Robert Keck, author of *Sacred Eyes*, "We have created a chasm between the sacred and the profane, heaven and earth, divine and human, spirit and matter, good and evil."[6] Because of this, we naturally have the perception that the Divine resides beyond ourselves in God or a Savior, and that humans, by comparison, are a pretty sorry lot.

By projecting attention outward away from ourselves rather than recognizing the divinity that God has put within each of us, we diminish all of humankind that is made in God's image. It also prevents us from developing our God-given potential by God's grace and help, which in turn keeps us from experiencing heaven to its fullest. This low view of humankind also makes it possible to label some people as trash, sinners, lost, ungodly, hopeless, unworthy of heaven, and deserving of hell. With that understanding, without a tear in their eyes, some people feel completely justified when they mentally consign certain others to hell forever.

What a difference it makes when we can really grasp that God has made each one of us to be very special, and understand that we are all his precious children, made in God's image and partakers of the divine nature. Then we will not be able to tolerate the thought of one lost soul. Then the tears will flow from our eyes as they did from Jesus when he wept over the city of Jerusalem (Luke 19:41). Then we will not be content until the last precious soul has entered heaven. We will join in spirit with the good shepherd who wasn't content that 99 out of his hundred sheep were safe, but kept looking until the last one was found (Luke 15:3-7).

Finally, we will then be able to understand why the father of the prodigal son kept longing, yearning and looking for his lost son to come home. When he finally arrived home he said, "'Quickly, bring out a robe - the best one - and put it on him; put a ring on his finger and sandals on his feet. And get the fatted calf and kill it, and let us eat and celebrate; for this son of mine was dead and is alive again; he was lost and is found!'" (Luke 15:22-24).

Chapter Six

FREE AT LAST

From Hell To Heaven - How It Is Accomplished

It is important for us to clearly understand what would be involved in moving from an existence in hell to an eternity in heaven. I caution you against thinking that, if getting out of hell is an option and if everyone is eventually going to be saved anyway, you can live it up now, because if you do end up in hell, you will easily be able to just leave and find your way to heaven. I must strongly emphasize that you cannot get out of hell in the same way as if you were traveling from one town to another. You cannot leave hell in that sense. In fact, you cannot leave hell any more than you can leave yourself. That is because hell is not so much a place as it is a spiritual state of being.

Heaven and Hell - Spiritual States of Being

The environment of hell is not necessarily different from that of heaven, but what one does within it is what makes it heaven or hell. People commonly have the impression that dying and going to heaven is like moving to Hawaii. The assumption is that one could not help but be happy while living in such a paradise. If we give it some thought, however, we will realize such a scenario really could not be true. There are unhappy people in Hawaii, as is true any place else. And there are people living in severe climates who experience great happiness and fulfillment. So it is not particularly relevant what the environment is like in heaven, or hell.

Hell, as a spiritual state of being, is characterized by such things as hatred, selfishness, greed, revenge, anger, feuding and power struggles. By everyone living according to those standards it makes it hell for everybody living there. What follows is weeping and gnashing of teeth. The real issue is not that people will exist in hell, but that hell will exist within them. So the reason you cannot leave hell anymore than you can leave yourself is because that which makes it hell comes from inside you.

We can appropriately conclude that God did not create hell as if it were in a geographical location such as Siberia where a person might be sent for punishment. It is more accurate to consider hell the creation of sinners, because sinfulness results in misery. I believe that no one is sent to hell to be punished for his or her sins. Hell is merely the natural consequence of the behavior with which we hurt others or ourselves. When we hurt others, the pain eventually comes back to cause misery for ourselves.

Consider the parable of the rich man and Lazarus (Luke 16:19-31). Those who believe that once one goes to hell he or she is there to stay forever typically place great emphasis on this passage in defense of their position. Rather than focusing on just the one main point of the parable (which is; those who make riches and self-indulgence their god, will experience hell), they focus on each detail. Where it reads, "Between you and us a great chasm has been fixed, so that those who might want to pass from here to you cannot do so, and no one can cross from there to us," they interpret it to refer to physically and literally moving from one place to another.

Again, it is important to realize that heaven and hell are not so much places as they are spiritual states of being. With that in mind, we can better understand why the people in the parable were not able to go between heaven and hell. That is because the chasm in this parable does not refer to a deep gorge in the ground as much as it represents the difference between the spiritual states of heaven and hell. With that understanding, the only way Lazarus could have gone to hell to give some comfort to the rich man was to have reverted to the spiritual state of being (characterized by turning one's back on God and acting in ways, such as; hateful, selfish and greedy) which would cause him to experience hell. Since Lazarus loved God, that would have been impossible for him to do. In that sense, therefore, it was impossible for him to go to hell to comfort the rich man.

Conversely, the rich man also could not literally, physically go from hell to heaven. But, it is of interest and great significance that, in the parable, we see change already beginning to take place in the rich man. At the end of the parable, the rich man was expressing genuine concern about his brothers, while before; he apparently wasn't concerned about anyone but himself. He showed he cared by asking Lazarus to warn his brothers so they would not end up in hell along with him. That is progress, which if continued, could eventually result in the rich man's transformation into the spiritual state of being through which he would experience heaven.

Another way to illustrate the chasm that existed between the rich man and Lazarus is with the following story, as told by Leslie Weatherhead:

Two men go to a concert of classical music. One is a musician to his finger tips. He has given hours to studying and practicing music. Every phrase of the music gives him delight, and in the concert he is, as we say, in the seventh heaven. His friend is frankly bored. He has never liked music, never taken any interest in it. He longs for the intermission. He can enter into *its* delights! They sit together, but between them there is a great gulf. And it is "fixed," for the musician cannot, however desirous, bring his friend into the bliss which his appreciation of music has made possible for him. At the same time the unmusical man *can begin to learn music.*[1]

Change That Results in Heaven

While you cannot leave hell as if you were going from one geographical location to another, you can get out of hell in another sense. You can be delivered from hell by allowing God to change what is within you, to turn you around so that your existence will be characterized not by hatred but love; not by selfishness but selflessness; not by greed but generosity; not by revenge but forgiveness; not by anger but compassion; not by feuding but peace; and not by power struggles, but by submitting to God's power. When a person is changed in that way, or turned around (converted), he or she will no longer experience hell but heaven.

This kind of change is not something that happens automatically or easily. For one thing, people have a sinful nature that causes them to go astray and seek life from other gods. Some of these gods are obvious, such as materialism, power and pleasure. Other less obvious gods from which we might seek fullness in this life could be worthwhile causes or relationships with other people. This is not to suggest that we should not pursue worthwhile causes and relationships with others. It is just that if we depend on them for ultimate fulfillment and life, they will sometimes let us down.

Original Sin - Laziness

Our sinful nature is the reality of what is commonly referred to as original sin. I have had a hard time making much sense out of that idea. I have never been able to understand how sin having been committed by Adam and Eve would somehow corrupt all of humankind and cause everyone since then to be sinners. The fifth century theologian, Augustine, tried to make sense out of the concept of original sin by suggesting that it was, in effect, a kind of venereal disease passed down through a man's seed. That would explain how Jesus, having been conceived by the Holy Spirit, could have avoided contracting original sin. That explanation is not too helpful to me. That is because I believe sinfulness is not the result of a genetic flaw, but is a spiritual matter.

So what can we make of this idea of original sin? How can we understand it? Sin is sadly a reality for all of us. M. Scott Peck, in his book, *The Road Less Traveled*, offers the best explanation I have come across. He contends that original sin is our laziness. He says, "we are all lazy to some extent. No matter how energetic, ambitious or even wise we may be, if we truly look into ourselves we will find laziness lurking at some level. It is the force of entropy within us, pushing us down and holding us all back from our spiritual evolution."[2] Peck goes to the extent of suggesting, "laziness in the form of our sick self might even be the devil."[3]

Regardless of how we understand original sin or the devil, we can probably all agree that sin and evil are realities which sometimes keep us from doing what is right, and prevent us from allowing God to transform us. I am convinced that laziness is a major contributing factor in this regard. Because of laziness, we tend to fear and resist change or new information. That is because it requires a good deal of work to change our perception of reality and the way we act. Maintaining the status quo or even regressing is very compelling. Neither of those requires work. They appeal to our sense of laziness (our sinful nature). Growing, maturing, becoming transformed puts a lot of responsibility upon us, and yes, requires work. It is easier and much more appealing for some of us to put all the responsibility on God, who we believe may condemn us or reward us. But at least it doesn't require us to do anything difficult like change, grow, or incorporate new ideas into our view of life.

There are many other factors, such as pride, self-idolatry, stubbornness, and misguidance, which combine with laziness to result in the experience of hell. They cause people to be deceived and led astray from God's purposes for life. As long as this deception continues to influence us, it will be no easier to get out of hell than it is to get out of a vicious cycle of revenge or to conquer a drug addiction.

There Is Hope

Even with all that is against us, there is hope. This hope is in the power of an all-loving God, one who is much more powerful than any influence of evil upon us or our misguided nature. Whether it happens in this life or the next, people will eventually realize that their false gods have failed them; that instead of giving them fullness of life, and the promise of eternal life, their gods' failures have left them with despair and meaninglessness (hell). When that happens, people will become receptive to the one true God who will then lead them home to be with God, where they will experience eternal life. (Incidentally, that same process, which is conversion, takes place in this life as well as the next.)

For people who have not been converted in this life, the conversion process may take some time; an hour, a day, a year; perhaps a hundred years, or even longer. But I believe God will eventually prevail. God will help everyone see the light, and thereby draw them out of hell. God wants everybody to be saved. And I believe God will eventually succeed in saving everyone, more likely sooner than later.

Prepare for Heaven

Let us think more about the consequences of our behavior. Let no one be deceived. Living in an evil way does not give us the best of this life or the next. It brings misery. Ultimately, it is hell. Besides, living according to evil standards actually prepares us for hell instead of heaven.

It would be wiser for us to establish patterns of life and values that prepare us for life in heaven. If we, for example, put all of our time and energy into getting rich, achieving academic accomplishments, climbing the social ladder, or doing better than the Joneses, it will not prepare us for heaven. If, on the other hand, we put our emphasis on endeavors, such as; trying to serve other people, comforting the distressed, helping those who are troubled and working for the unity of all humankind, we will become prepared to fit right into heaven in the next world. It does not make sense to subject us to the misery of hell at all, in this life or the next. So we are all well advised to humbly and faithfully serve God and help others now, and to allow God to give us victory in life. Then we will experience a degree of heaven in this life and become prepared to experience the fullness of heaven in the next life as well.

The Command to Love

A Pharisee had asked Jesus which was the greatest commandment in the law. Jesus replied, "'You shall love the Lord your God with all your heart, and with all your soul, and with all your mind.' This is the greatest and first commandment. And a second is like it: 'You shall love your neighbor as yourself'" (Matthew 22:37-39).

This is the most basic teaching in Christianity. Love. When we love God and others we will experience the joy of their love and goodwill in return. That is the essence of salvation. It is eternal life. It is heaven, in this life and the next. On the other hand, living in a self-centered way, caring neither for God nor others is what it means to be lost. Such a life would cause us to experience hell, in this life and the next.

As we grow in our love for God and others, we will come to realize that the ultimate expression of love is to love our enemies. An impossible task, you might think, when you read Jesus as quoted in Matthew 5:43-45: "You have heard that it was said, 'you shall love your neighbor and hate your enemy.' But I say to you, Love your enemies and pray for those who persecute you, so that you may be children of your Father in heaven; for he makes his sun rise on the evil and on the good, and sends rain on the righteous and on the unrighteous." To seemingly make matters worse, this passage concludes with, "Be perfect, therefore, as your heavenly Father is perfect" (Matthew 5:48).

At first it may seem like there is no obvious connection between this concluding verse and the rest of the foregoing passage. First it says God is accepting of everyone, the evil as well as the good. Then it suggests we need to be perfect in order to be acceptable. Walter Wink (seminary professor and author), however, says, "Jesus could not have said, 'Be perfect.' There is no such word, or even concept, in Aramaic or Hebrew."[4]

Rather than describing moral perfection, "perfect" was an aesthetic term that could be used to describe a geometric form, for instance. In understanding the literal intent of the word within the context of this entire passage, it becomes clear that when Jesus says we are to behave like God, he is not saying that we are to be morally perfect (which is impossible). Instead, we are to mimic God in our love for even those who are least worthy of our love, our enemies. Loving even our enemies is entirely possible because Jesus calls and empowers us to embrace everyone. He is not calling us to an impossible perfection. As by grace we grow in God's love, we begin to understand that by recognizing and accepting our own imperfection, failures, and sinfulness, we will become enabled to embrace those whom we feel are least perfect, least deserving, and most threatening to us. We are to love God and others, even our enemies, and thus, experience salvation. Loving in that way demonstrates we have truly been converted.

That leads me to ask, what is the primary purpose of Christian conversion? It seems to me that most people believe the main reason we need to be converted is in order to get into heaven. I disagree. I believe the primary purpose of Christian conversion is to enable us to love as God loves. We naturally love those who love us, our family and friends. But Jesus says, "If you love those who love you, what reward do you have? Do not even the tax collectors do the same?" (Matthew 5:45). Christians are distinguished from the rest of humanity not because they are destined for heaven but because they have been empowered to love in a new way, to love strangers, persecutors, enemies, and the unlovable. If we learn to love in that way, the question of whether or not we will go to heaven will be of little significance. We will already be there.

About-Face
The difference between an existence in heaven and one in

hell is determined by the direction we are facing spiritually. Jeremiah 2:27 reads; "They have turned their backs on me, and not their faces." Those of us who are following God's ways are ultimately being drawn into an ever closer spiritual fellowship with God and those around us, and are thus experiencing heaven. Those who have turned away from God and the love of others to live a life concerned only with themselves experience the hell of alienation.

Some in heaven experience a greater degree of joy and fulfillment than others, depending on how close they have grown to God and those around them. By the same token, the degree of misery that one may experience in hell is determined by how far one has degenerated into the hell of self-indulgence, jealousy and revenge. Heaven and hell are not fixed states experienced by everyone in the same way. Instead, they are dynamic and changing, with each individual moving along a continuum of joy and pain, either closer to or further from the love of God and others.

To be drawn by God from hell to heaven is to allow oneself to be turned around (converted). This results in a person's removal from the continuum of hell, where people have turned their backs on God and others, to be placed on the continuum of heaven, where they experience the joy of face-to-face, loving encounters with God and others. It is like traveling home by way of an interstate highway when you realize you have taken a wrong turn, which resulted in your heading in the opposite direction from what you intended. To make matters worse, you are approaching dangerous storm clouds. You take the first opportunity to cross the median and head back the other way. Soon the sun is shining. What a joy it is to be on the way home!

That is the kind of change that places a person on the way of Jesus, who said, "I am the way. . . to the Father" (John 14:6), and identifies one with those "belonging to the Way" (Acts 9:2). The term, "the Way", suggests that there is no immediate and complete transformation, causing the person to have arrived. But it places the person on the right track, facing in the right direction, to begin an eternity of growth in grace. And what an adventure that is, as we experience more and more of God's grace and love!

We will address this great opportunity for growth in chapter eight.

Chapter Seven

GOING BEYOND WISHFUL THINKING

The Power of Unconditional Love

What great news we have! We will all eventually be converted, transformed, and enabled to live in a new way so that we and those we influence will be able to experience heaven to the fullest. You might wonder what dynamics of God's power can accomplish such a feat. I assure you it does not happen by chance or mystical magic beyond our comprehension. It is also not accomplished by what is commonly perceived to be powerful; that which is imposing, threatening, controlling, dominating, or by power of a military nature. So what is this power which takes us beyond merely wishing for the salvation of everyone? It is the power of unconditional love.

To identify the powerful love into which we are called, the writers of the New Testament used the Greek word *agape*. *Agape* is spiritual love of one person for another, corresponding to the love of God for people. It is unselfish love for others without sexual implications. It is no small thing to experience *agape* love.

Unconditional Love Is Essential
The teaching of eternal damnation makes it impossible for

us to believe that God loves us unconditionally. If we believe God consigns some people to hell forever, or simply abandons them in their misery, could we say with any conviction that God has unconditional love for us?

If we believe in eternal damnation, wouldn't that also mean we believe there is no such thing as unconditional love? If we think God lacks the capacity to love unconditionally, how could any of us be so presumptuous as to expect to express it to others ourselves? Surely none of us would believe we are superior to God in the purity of our love. The teaching of eternal damnation eliminates the possibility of unconditional love on the part of God or ourselves, but isn't unconditional love exactly what we want and need in our lives?

If, on the other hand, we embrace the teaching of universal salvation, haven't we recognized that unconditional love is not only possible, but that it is the force that is essential to bring about the salvation of everyone?

Someone who does not understand the power of love might suggest that if God loves us unconditionally, that would indicate God is soft on sin. God is not soft on sin. Paradoxically, that does not mean we must be free of sin as a prerequisite for receiving God's unconditional love. Obviously, if sinlessness or any other requirement were a condition for receiving God's love, that love would not be unconditional.

I trust it is becoming very clear that just because God is unconditionally loving and accepting, it does not mean that our behavior lacks importance. There still remain standards of right and wrong. Standards and behavior matter enormously. But rather than deserving love because we are righteous, it is precisely our condition as sinners which makes unconditional love essential. Only by its power and influence are people transformed to higher and higher standards.

What power is there in "be-good-and-you'll-be-rewarded religion" or "don't-be-bad-or-you'll-be-punished religion"? Either type provides us with only external motivation. Neither one brings about change within a person. Those kinds of religion amount to bargaining with God, and you get only what you bargained for. In contrast, there is enormous power in a "you-are-loved-unconditionally faith". The significance of this belief is that it has the power to transform each of us. The resulting internal changes provide the foundation for our new, victorious lives.

I realize this goes against conventional wisdom, which contends that God must punish evildoers. But that is not God's way. God's way is to unconditionally love evildoers.

Jesus' Transforming Unconditional Love

Unconditional love and acceptance is precisely what Jesus taught and demonstrated while he walked among us. Jesus was accepting, loving and forgiving (to a fault, as the Pharisees saw it). One day some people took a paralyzed man to Jesus so that Jesus might heal him. Even before he healed the man physically, Jesus said, "Friend, your sins are forgiven you" (Luke 5:20). What an amazing and revolutionary thing to do! He pronounced the man forgiven even before he had a chance to repent or do anything else to show he deserved forgiveness. Wasn't that just like Jesus? As a result of actions such as this, sinners were empowered to live as forgiven people. Think of the implications! What might happen if we acted toward others in the same way?

One day while Jesus passed through Jericho a man named Zacchaeus climbed up in a tree in order to get a better look at Jesus. As Jesus approached, he looked up and said,

"Zacchaeus, hurry and come down; for I must stay at your house today." [6]So he hurried down and was happy to welcome him. [7]All who saw it began to grumble and said, "He has gone to be the guest of one who is a sinner." [8]Zacchaeus stood there and said to the Lord, "Look, half of my possessions, Lord, I will give to the poor; and if I have defrauded anyone of anything, I will pay back four times as much." [9]Then Jesus said to him, "Today salvation has come to this house." (Luke 19:5-9)

Zacchaeus' reaction to Jesus' unconditional love and

acceptance was remarkable. Jesus had not accused him of fraud or told him he must give away his possessions. But Zacchaeus spontaneously responded as a changed man. There truly is great power in unconditional love.

Jesus became close friends with many of the outcasts of society. He spent much time with them, which was scandalous to the religious leaders of the day. Luke 15:1-2 reads; "Now all the tax collectors and sinners were coming near to listen to (Jesus). And the Pharisees and the scribes were grumbling and saying, 'This fellow welcomes sinners and eats with them.'" While Jesus' behavior was offensive to some, it had a powerful, positive affect on many people he encountered. According to Luke 7:36-50,

> [36]One of the Pharisees asked Jesus to eat with him, and he went into the Pharisee's house and took his place at the table. [37]And a woman in the city, having learned that he was eating at the Pharisee's house, brought an alabaster jar of ointment. [38]She stood behind him at his feet, weeping, and began to bathe his feet with her tears and to dry them with her hair. Then she continued kissing his feet and anointing them with the ointment. [39]Now when the Pharisee who had invited him saw it, he said to himself, "If this man were a prophet, he would have known who and what kind of woman this is who is touching him - that she is a sinner." [40]Jesus spoke up and said to him, "Simon, I have something to say to you." "Teacher," he replied, "Speak." [41]"A certain creditor had two debtors; one owed five hundred denarii, and the other fifty. [42]When they could not pay, he canceled the debts of both of them. Now which of them will love him more?" [43]Simon answered, "I suppose the one for whom he canceled the greater debt." And Jesus said to him, "You have judged rightly." [44]Then turning toward the woman, he said to Simon, "Do you see this woman? I entered your house; you gave me no water for my feet, but she has bathed my feet with her tears and dried

them with her hair. ⁴⁵You gave me no kiss, but from the time I came in she has not stopped kissing my feet. ⁴⁶You did not anoint my head with oil, but she has anointed my feet with ointment. ⁴⁷Therefore, I tell you, her sins, which were many, have been forgiven; hence she has shown great love. But the one to whom little is forgiven, loves little." ⁴⁸Then he said to her, "Your sins are forgiven." ⁴⁹But those who were at the table with him began to say among themselves, "Who is this who even forgives sins?" ⁵⁰And he said to the woman, "Your faith has saved you; go in peace."

On another occasion, a woman who had been caught in adultery was brought before Jesus. The scribes and Pharisees made her stand before all of them, then said to Jesus,

"Teacher, this woman was caught in the very act of committing adultery. ⁵Now in the law Moses commanded us to stone such a woman. Now what do you say?" ⁶They said this to test him, so that they might have some charge to bring against him. Jesus bent down and wrote with his finger on the ground. ⁷When they kept on questioning him, he straightened up and said to them, "Let anyone among you who is without sin be the first to throw a stone at her." ⁸And once again he bent down and wrote on the ground. ⁹When they heard it, they went away, one by one, beginning with the elders; and Jesus was left alone with the woman standing before him. ¹⁰Jesus straightened up and said to her, "Woman, where are they? Has no one condemned you?" ¹¹She said, "No one, sir." And Jesus said, "Neither do I condemn you. Go your way, and from now on do not sin again" (John 8:4-11).

If Jesus had condemned and scolded this woman how do you think she might have responded? I do not believe it would have been favorable. She knew she was guilty. She did not need Jesus to tell her so. In order to be healed of her broken condition she needed, not judgment, but acceptance, compassion and forgiveness. That is exactly what Jesus gave her. And we have every reason to believe that through that loving encounter, the woman was empowered to live in a new and positive way.

What of those who would have stoned the woman? Jesus did not glare at them or confront them. Instead, he busied himself by writing in the sand, which gave the woman's accusers the time to look into their own hearts. They found themselves wanting. Jesus had given them his unconditional love and acceptance as well.

While the above examples are very significant, the most powerful manifestation of Jesus' unconditional love was demonstrated not in the way he lived but in the manner in which he died. While Jesus was loved and accepted by many people, others ridiculed, spit upon, whipped, and ultimately, crucified him. What was his response as they did those things to him? He forgave them! He prayed for those who crucified him, saying, "Father, forgive them; for they do not know what they are doing" (Luke 23:34). His forgiveness had a powerful, eye opening impact on many people, including the Roman centurion who was in charge of the crucifixion. After Jesus died, "when the centurion, who stood facing him, saw that in this way he breathed his last, he said, 'Truly this man was God's Son!'" (Mark 15:39).

Jesus forgave them all. What a power-packed expression of unconditional love! Jesus' enemies did not have the last word. The ways of Jesus prevailed. He achieved victory over sin, death, and the power of evil, not only for himself but also for all of humankind. If Jesus had cursed those who crucified him, they would have felt justified in killing him. There would have been no power in his death. His death would have ended his influence. The Christian Church would never have come into existence. Jesus, however, did not curse his crucifiers, he loved them, prayed for them and forgave them. And as the saying goes, the rest is history. No one has influenced history as much as Jesus because of the very way he lived, and died. The power of Jesus' crucifixion has resulted in the conversion and transformation of billions of people over the centuries.

The Non-judgmental Nature of God

The opposite of the expression of unconditional love and acceptance is the passing of judgment upon others. Jesus said, "Do not judge, so that you may not be judged" (Matthew 7:1). It is well established in the Bible that we are not to be judgmental. The Bible makes clear to us the fact that Jesus was non-judgmental. He forgave people even before they repented, as has been illustrated earlier. According to John 12:47 Jesus said, "I do not judge anyone who hears my words and does not keep them, for I came not to judge the world, but to save the world."

It is clear to me that this non-judgmental picture of Jesus stands in stark contrast to the way many people continue to perceive God. They still think of God as one who records people's good and bad behavior, then ultimately sits on his throne in judgment to determine whether they go to heaven or hell.

You might ask, "How can there be such a difference between Jesus and God?" After all, Jesus said, "If you know me, you will know my Father also. From now on you do know him and have seen him" (John 14:7). The reason Jesus could claim to be the manifestation as well as the ultimate authority on God the Father is because he is the only one who has actually ever seen God, as indicated in John 1:18: "No one has ever seen God. It is God the only Son, who is close to the Father's heart, who has made him known." Also, John 6:46 reads, "Not that anyone has seen the Father except the one who is from God; He has seen the Father." Jesus is not judgmental. He is close to the Father's heart. He said that to know him is the same as knowing the Father. So can we really believe God is judgmental?

Clearly, this is a case where the Bible seems to speak with more than one voice. It is true that there are numerous passages in the Bible that refer to God as a judge. But is God judgmental? Or is God like Jesus? For me personally, this is an easy choice. When there is a difference between what Jesus said or personified and what is said elsewhere in the Bible, I'll go with Jesus without hesitation.

There may not be as much of a contrast as there may seem between Jesus and God when it comes to the issue of judgmentalism. It should not surprise us that the Biblical writers portrayed God as judgmental. It was natural that they would feel judged, guilty, inadequate, unholy, sinful and unworthy when they encountered the Holy. I believe that projection of feelings on the part of some of the writers of the Bible explains why God is portrayed as a judge, in contrast to the non-judgmental perception of Jesus. When we feel judged, we also have a natural tendency to project our feelings onto God and think of God as a judge, all the while judging ourselves.

Jesus has been described as a window through which we can look to see God. I like that concept. When Jesus says, "Father, forgive them; for they do not know what they are doing," he is speaking from the very heart of God. And God is one who would also tell a person who is guilty of adultery, "Neither do I condemn you." God speaks to each of us when we have gone astray, are lonely or troubled. If you listen, you might hear God say, "Come to me, my precious child. You are always welcome with me. I love you unconditionally, and always will."

The common perception of judgment is that it is negative. I believe that to feel judged by God is positive. Through judgment, God leads us forward on our spiritual journey. It is healthy and essential for salvation to recognize our shortcomings, and as a result, seek to be forgiven and transformed. Judgment is not the end. Instead, it makes possible a wonderful new beginning. God is with us to lovingly lead us into our new life.

Risk and Power in Following Jesus

Jesus calls us to follow his example and love others in a special way, to love them no matter what. I believe that is what he was talking about when he said, "If any want to become my followers, let them deny themselves and take up their cross daily and follow me" (Luke 9:23). It is a risky and difficult business to love others unconditionally, as Jesus taught us.

To love unconditionally puts us at risk of being treated like a doormat. We might ask, what is to prevent others from walking all over us? Abusing us? Taking advantage of us? Let's not forget the example of Jesus in this regard. He too was abused and eventually killed. But he was not defeated. He achieved the ultimate victory. The same redemptive and transforming dynamics that enabled Jesus to exert a powerfully positive influence on many people are available to each of us in the way we might choose to treat each other.

In forgiving those who crucified him, Jesus also demonstrated for us that by forgiving others who have wronged us, we take away any power they may have over us. Tremendous power for redemption and transformation results from our own undeserved suffering, while we continue to unconditionally love, accept and forgive those who impose the suffering.

The reason that to love and forgive those who inflict undeserved suffering upon us is so powerful is because it prevents defensiveness while it fosters repentance. If one strikes back at a perpetrator of injustice, the perpetrator will naturally become defensive and a confrontation may likely ensue. But if one continues to love and forgive an aggressor, that love and forgiveness can result in self-examination by the guilty party. The feeling of guilt over the unjust infliction of pain upon you, an innocent person, leads that perpetrator to repent and to seek forgiveness. Often the result is a dramatic and positive internal change in that individual.

We may fear the prospect of how we might be treated if we give others the gift of unconditional love. It can be a crucifying experience. But just think of the continuous infusion of vitality and meaningfulness into our lives as we by God's grace and power daily take up such a cross and follow Jesus! Think of the lives of others that will be transformed! There is enormous power in living as a radical lover, like Jesus.

If, on the other hand, we fail to follow Jesus' example and are judgmental, critical and unforgiving, and place conditions on our love and acceptance of others, the consequences could be devastating. We learn what those negative effects can be by observing the lives of others as well as by examining what we may experience ourselves. If we believe there are conditions upon which we ourselves will be loved and accepted, we find ourselves constantly burdened with trying to prove ourselves worthy. How painful it is to feel we do not measure up, and to be convinced that we probably never will.

It is bad enough as a child to feel that you can never please your parents. It is much worse to believe that you are not, and probably never will be, good enough to earn God's favor. Though people will tell us God loves us, they will sometimes go on to say that anything less than perfection falls short of God's expectations. How can we ever hope to please God if that is the case?

The deprivation of unconditional love and acceptance destroys our self-esteem. We may manifest this in our withdrawal from humanity or become painfully shy, or unable to deal honestly with or to trust others. We might grow arrogant, judgmental, and critical of others and ourselves. In contrast, when we receive unconditional love and acceptance, our self-esteem is built up. It is then possible for us to feel non-judgmental of ourselves, which in turn helps us to respect others and accept them just as they are.

Offering support to others is essential if we are to have a positive influence on them. Criticism defeats people and crushes their spirits, while unconditional acceptance builds them up. We all need to be told we are doing the best we can under the circumstances of our lives. We need to let other people know that where they stand in their spiritual journey at any particular moment is all right with us, and with God.

We do not have to do all things perfectly. When we demand perfection from ourselves it is inevitably self-defeating. But when we receive acceptance, support and encouragement at all times, we are empowered to go on to eventually exceed even our own greatest hopes, dreams and expectations, spiritually and in every other aspect of our lives. What power there is in loving and accepting someone else unconditionally! And what big benefits come from it!

Jesus said, "You shall love (agape) your neighbor as yourself" (Matthew 22:39). That tells us that to love others is possible if we love ourselves. We can carry this idea a step further and realize it is only when we love ourselves unconditionally that we are able to love others unconditionally as well. Sadly, this does not always come naturally for us. But Melody Beattie, author of *The Language of Letting Go*, tells us how we can learn to love ourselves without conditions;

How do we love ourselves? By forcing it at first. By faking it if necessary. By "acting as if." By working as hard at loving and liking ourselves as we have at not liking ourselves.

Explore what it means to love yourself.

Do things for yourself that reflect compassion, nurturing, self-love.

Embrace and love all of yourself - past, present, and future. Forgive yourself quickly and as often as necessary. Encourage yourself. Tell yourself good things about yourself. . . .

We work at it, then work at it some more. One day we'll wake up, look in the mirror, and find that loving ourselves has become habitual. We're now living with a person who gives and receives love, because that person loves him-or herself. Self-love will take hold and become a guiding force in our life.[1]

What a good description Beattie has provided of what it takes to love oneself and its meaning! Self-love is wonderful and essential for a healthy, full and happy life. How blessed we are when we learn to love ourselves unconditionally. We are then in a position to have a life-transforming influence on others after we learn to love them unconditionally as well.

Passive and Assertive Expressions
of Unconditional Love

The expression of unconditional love can be manifested in passive as well as assertive ways. The effectiveness of these manners of influence upon others is determined by the personalities of their recipients. The passive expression of unconditional love and acceptance has a powerful effect on anyone. But the transforming influence takes place much more quickly with some people than others. Gradual change and growth is fine in most cases, but there are those situations such as where a person may be at risk of harming himself or others, when acting more assertively is in order. In such cases, parents, for example, may impose a variety of sanctions on their children, even sometimes implementing extreme measures.

Let us remember that, while disciplining children or imposing sanctions on others, we are effective only to the extent that we do so with love and respect. If our actions are motivated by anger or the desire for revenge, the results are more likely to be negative than positive. If we act in love, especially unconditional love, the potential for positive benefits is unlimited.

When I worked at the Iowa State Juvenile Home in Toledo, Iowa, we dealt with a great variety of young people, all with different needs. Some of them responded magnificently to passive expressions of unconditional love. With others, we had to be more assertive. I'm sure at times the youth felt we had been pretty tough on them. Most importantly though, we had a wonderful staff who treated the residents in such a way that they knew they were both loved and respected. Because of this fact, virtually all of the young people experienced significant growth while they resided at the home.

As we looked back, it became very evident to all of us on the staff that those who were the hardest to love were the ones who needed unconditional love the most. Of course, God knew that better than we did. So I believe that for those who were the least lovable and, therefore, the most difficult to love, God made a special point of helping us to do the best we could in giving them a full, continuous dose of unconditional love.

Loving others unconditionally sometimes involves giving them guidance and helping them to see the error of their ways. There are times when people really do not realize they are doing something wrong. In those cases, the loving thing is to help them become aware.

Jesus had several encounters with the scribes and Pharisees, some of whom were very self-righteous. On more than one occasion Jesus called them hypocrites. That sounds rather harsh, and it is. But indications are they had no idea they were hypocritical, so apparently calling it to their attention was the kind of confrontation they needed to become aware of their faults. While Jesus unconditionally loved and accepted them, he also firmly but compassionately helped them see their shortcomings.

The key to helping a person realize he is in error so we can help bring about positive change and growth is not to attack him but to ask pertinent questions and offer supportive suggestions when he is receptive to them. All this is done within the context of loving and accepting him just as he is.

The power of a positive example is another essential ingredient in exerting a favorable influence upon others. If we display anger and unforgiveness, how can we expect others to rise above that same kind of behavior? Since love is contagious, if we truly love, others are likely to catch love from us, aren't they?

Putting Everything into God's Hands

I do not suggest that a person should passively let others abuse him or her, or that one should not protest or resist abuse, or that one should stay in a situation in which continued abuse is likely. What I do say is that, even in the most trying of circumstances, we need to continue to give unconditional love because in many situations, unconditional love, acceptance and forgiveness are the only forces powerful enough to penetrate the defenses and bring about transformation for a person desperately in need of help.

Unconditional love is an awesome power. But even it cannot always bring about immediate change. With all that we may do in our endeavor to love others and effect a positive influence upon them, they may not always respond as positively or quickly as we would like them to. Instead, they may shut our love out of their lives. When that happens, we need to continue to love them unconditionally anyway, and to put the whole situation into God's hands. In Melody Beattie's words, "We detach with the understanding that life is unfolding exactly as it needs to, for others and ourselves. . . .We do this with the understanding that a Power greater than ourselves is in charge and all is well."[2]

With this perspective we can be at peace, knowing that when the time is right, when the person is ready, by the grace of God he will be motivated and empowered to leave behind the darkness, cold and pain. He will begin to experience instead, the light, warmth, healing and fullness of life.

Unconditional Love and Miracles

With Jesus as our teacher, we learn that love is not really love unless it is unconditional. According to 1 John 4:19, "We love (agape) because (God) first loved (agape) us." That's the way it works. Love fosters love, and unconditional love brings forth unconditional love in its recipients. If we expect people to earn our love, we will always find a reason to feel disappointed. There will always remain an unrealized expectation. But when we give unconditional love, miracles begin to happen.

We might initially think that by loving others unconditionally we run the risk of giving them permission to continue to sin. This assumption might lead us to ask, why would a person change for the better if he knew he was going to be fully loved and accepted regardless of his actions? In her book entitled, *A Return To Love*, Marianne Williamson answers,

> Accepting people as they are has the miraculous effect of helping them improve. Acceptance doesn't

prohibit growth; rather, it fosters it.

People who are always telling us what's wrong with us don't help us so much as they paralyze us with shame and guilt. People who accept us help us to feel good about ourselves, to relax, to find our way.[3]

The reason criticism of others has the negative influence that it does is because people usually already know when they are in the wrong. They do not need someone else to tell them. Besides, the way people are often told what is wrong with them comes in the form of an attack rather than as a supportive, constructive suggestion. When a person feels attacked, his natural response is to defend himself, and perhaps even strike back. Not surprisingly, that kind of encounter seldom brings about a positive change. Indeed, it often makes matters worse. We can all think of times we might have handled a situation better.

On the other hand, it is natural for us to respond with appreciation and love for the one who is not judgmental, but supportive. That results in other valuable benefits for us. The mere presence of someone who loves and accepts us just as we are compels us to convict ourselves by our own sense of guilt. That change of heart brings about our repentance, forgiveness from others, and ultimately the process of transformation, through which we learn to love and forgive others and ourselves.

There are numerous Biblical examples of the miraculous effects of total acceptance, such as; the stories of Zacchaeus (Luke 19:1-10), and of the woman who wet Jesus' feet with her tears and dried them with her hair (Luke 7:36-50).

When we learn to love unconditionally, we will be able to stop acting judgmentally and critically of others. That is because we will interpret all of their responses to us, whether positive or negative, as falling into one of two categories; either as an expression of love or as an appeal for love. With this perspective, we will be enabled to love all people in all circumstances.

How sad and tragic life would be without love. But, what

beauty, majesty, fullness, and vitality our lives hold when we experience an abundance of love in it, especially unconditional love. There is enormous power in unconditional love - power to change lives - power to change the world - power to make every child feel special, loved and valuable - power to equip every adult to live victoriously - power to eventually bring every lost person home to be with God.

Chapter Eight

FORGIVENESS IS ONLY THE BEGINNING

Growing Into God's Likeness

It is not sufficient for the eternal well being of our spirits to merely receive forgiveness of our sins, as important as that is. Growth beyond forgiveness is absolutely essential for us as Christians if we are to ever experience heaven to its fullest.

Going Beyond Forgiveness

One may pray a selfish prayer such as, "Dear God, please forgive my sins so I can go to heaven when I die." Do you think such a prayer would ring true to God? If a request for forgiveness is sincere, its focus will not be only on what's in it for us. It must be followed by a change of heart if it is to be truly meaningful. If it is not, it is a sham. If God forgave us because of our whim of a prayer, wouldn't that tell us God does not consider sin a serious problem? Wouldn't it amount to God saying, "There, there, I know you didn't mean it, and it really doesn't matter, so I forgive you"? Wouldn't that way of thinking take sin and our need for forgiveness and transformation far too lightly?

Forgiveness is not the end in itself. It is just the beginning of a new life. True, forgiveness is sufficient to help us begin to experience something of heaven and to be identified with

God's people. But if we continue to live as sinners, our actions will naturally bring misery to ourselves and others, including our loved ones. People must be sincerely changed, transformed and healed - in other words, made whole, if heaven is going to be heavenly in the fullest sense for everyone.

Healing

It is interesting that the words salvation and salve begin the same way. They both involve healing. We put salve on our skin to help heal a cut or infection. Salvation is the healing of our spirits. Healing was an integral part of Jesus' ministry. When some of the disciples of John the Baptist asked Jesus if he was the expected Messiah, he answered, "Go and tell John what you have seen and heard: the blind receive their sight, the lame walk, the lepers are cleansed, the deaf hear, the dead are raised, the poor have good news brought to them" (Luke 7:22). Jesus taught that healing was evidence of the nearness of God's kingdom, according to Luke 10:9, where he tells his disciples, "Cure the sick who are there, and say to them, 'The kingdom of God has come near to you.'"

Physical healing, while not synonymous with salvation, is an integral part of it. We, however, need to make it very clear that if a person is handicapped or ill and is not healed, it does not mean that person is not saved. Of course, we are all destined to die physically, so in that sense we will all eventually experience not being healed. Even in death, however, people will experience the ultimate in healing. "God himself will be with them; he will wipe every tear from their eyes. Death will be no more; mourning and crying and pain will be no more, for the first things have passed away" (Revelation 21:3-4).

Certainly, being healed and made whole emotionally and spiritually is at the heart of salvation. We need to affirm that if there is no healing in those respects there is ultimately no salvation. We must each be made into a new creation if we are ever going to be able to live together in such a way that all can experience heaven.

Becoming Fully Human

One way to express what our goal is in spiritual growth and healing is to say that God wants each of us to become fully human. I realize not everyone would equate becoming fully human with becoming everything God wants us to be, or with reaching our full growth potential. That is because we, in the Church, have for centuries placed so much emphasis on humankind's sinful nature as a way of trying to convince people of their desperate need to be saved. Consequently, many people entertain a decidedly low view of humankind. I believe this consequence of the Church's teachings is a travesty. After all, Jesus was human, fully human, and there was nothing wrong with him. He was not only morally perfect, but was the personification of God in the world.

During the early Church, there were some people who adhered to the doctrine of Docetism. They believed Jesus was divine and that he only appeared as a human. According to them he was not really one of us, but actually was God merely acting the part of being a human.[1] Docetism was rejected by most of the early Christians as they affirmed Jesus' full humanity, as well as his full divinity.

Unfortunately, Docetism still flourishes. People do not generally go to the extreme of denying Jesus' humanity entirely. But in my ministry I have seen that most people place greater emphasis on Jesus' divinity than his humanity, perhaps considering him about ninety-nine percent divine while being only one percent human. The problem with that idea is that it suggests we humans have very little in common with Jesus, in our nature or our potential.

We read of Jesus healing the sick, raising the dead, multiplying food to feed the hungry and loving his enemies. We also see him living a flawless life and praying for those who crucified him. Jesus did show in many ways that he was genuinely human, such as when he cried after his friend Lazarus died. Because he did so many great things, however, people still tend to believe they could never be like him or do many of the things he did.

Through degrading humanity we sell ourselves short and minimize what we might do by God's power. But Jesus has told us, "The one who believes in me will also do the works that I do and, in fact, will do greater works than these, because I am going to the Father. . . .If in my name you ask me for anything, I will do it" (John 14:12,14). So Jesus expects big things from us, as he works in us and through us.

In light of this, I believe that one way to describe the purpose of the Christian faith, or to understand what salvation is all about, is to make us fully or genuinely human, while at the same time, becoming more like God. That being the case, we can increasingly live in a truly human manner, while we also manifest more and more of the divinity that God has put within each of us.

I used to believe that to envision Jesus as both fully human and fully divine simultaneously was tantamount to mixing water and oil. I was told in confirmation class as a youth, in my reading of theological books and articles over the years, and even in seminary, that it was impossible to understand how that God/man phenomenon could take place. But it was considered very important to believe that Jesus was both human and divine. So this doctrine was just considered something to accept even though it was a mystery as to how it could be possible.

I have since come to realize Jesus' divinity/humanity may not be such a mystery after all. The Bible speaks in many places about humans being transformed to become more like God, but there is never a mention of them giving up their humanity. As we grow to become more like God, we do not become less human. We become more human.

Jesus was fully human while he was fully divine. It was not as if two incompatible substances were unnaturally bound together in one person. On the contrary, Jesus' life shows us that to be human is in many ways the same as to be divine. As we become more like God we will also become more fully human. As we grow to be more like Jesus, we too will be able to affirm and celebrate that the kingdom of God is within us, that we are one with the Father, that the Father is in us, and we are in the Father.

When someone does something wrong we often hear him use the worn excuse, "I'm only human." This does everyone a terrible disservice in the way it degrades humankind. The problem is not that we are human, but that we are not fully human. We need to realize we can affirm, "I am human!! And by God's grace, love, and power I expect to become more fully human everyday!!"

God is in us. God is the ground of our being. We are in God. That is what makes us human and humane. As we by God's grace and power experience spiritual growth in our quest to become more like God, we do not have to become something different. We need to become more fully what we already are - human.

Four Stages of Spiritual Growth

In trying to understand what it specifically means to grow spiritually, I have found noted psychologist and author, M. Scott Peck to be very helpful. In his book, *Further Along the Road Less Traveled*, he outlines four stages of spiritual growth. Following is a summary of those stages.[2]

People in stage one, *Chaotic/antisocial*, are characterized by an absence of spirituality and are unprincipled. Their lives are chaotic. In order to overcome the misery and chaos of their lives, some of them convert to stage two. In stage two, *Formal/institutional*, people depend upon the Church to govern their lives. The structure, dependability and predictability appeal to their need for stability, but God is viewed to be judgmental and to send some people to hell forever. Some people eventually begin to question the validity of the institutional church and certain teachings. At this point they have begun their conversion to spiritual stage three.

Those in stage three, *Skeptic/individual*, aren't religious in the usual sense, but are more advanced spiritually than people in stage two. They are invariably truth seekers. As they seek truth, and the pieces of the larger picture start to come together, they are beginning their conversion to stage four. People in stage four, *Mystical/communal*, are able to see the interconnectedness between all of life and God. They are comfortable in a world of paradoxes and mystery, in contrast to those in stage two who are very uncomfortable when things are not clearly delineated.

I have observed that not everyone experiences each stage with the same intensity. Children of stage four parents often have a great advantage in growing through the spiritual stages. Some of their earliest memories are those of going to church. They cannot remember when God was not an important part of their lives. Like children of stage two parents, they internalize the teachings of the Church and become self-disciplined individuals. They, however, are able to avoid much of the rigidity and narrowness of stage two because they have always been encouraged to ask questions and be receptive to new thoughts. As a result, they are likely to experience little of the rebelliousness typically associated with the transition from stage two to three. As they mature, because their spiritual stage four parents have modeled its principles to them since early childhood, these people often move quite easily and naturally through stage three to four.

Many people do not begin the process of spiritual growth until they are adults. When that is the case, it is possible to move quickly through the spiritual stages. Sadly, however, many people become stuck in a stage and stop growing.

Don't Get Stuck in a Lower Spiritual Stage

It is obviously in a person's best interest to grow beyond stage one. Unfortunately, some people are slow to make that transition. One obstacle that hinders them is what is perceived to be the negative side of stage two. While a person may be miserable in stage one, stage two may not seem to them to be much of an improvement. People tend to not want to associate with others they feel are judgmental or with a God whom they have been told may throw them into hell for an eternity. People in stage one generally have no knowledge of the liberating possibilities of stages three and four. That is because most churches as well as radio and television preachers focus only on the need to advance to stage two. In not realizing that there are opportunities for greater spiritual growth beyond stage two, some people choose to stay in stage one.

Then there are those who advance to stage two and stop growing, often without realizing that is the case. I have known many people who are stuck in stage two, even while they emphasize the importance of growth. They believe that they are growing spiritually, but their growth all takes place within stage two. They are terrified by the possibility that they may have doubts and questions. This to them suggests a lack of faith or commitment on their part. They will not let themselves entertain a skeptical thought. They allow themselves only to think and do what they have been taught to think and do. They find security in pat answers. They need things to be spelled out in very clear terms. Without realizing it, these people are in a rut. Growth for them does not involve expanding the rut but only in digging it deeper. If people at that place in their spiritual development are ever going to move on to stages three and four, they are going to have to muster the courage to peek out over the sides of their rut and begin to explore the broader world.

A person staying within the confines of stage two is like a butterfly remaining inside its cocoon. Living in a cocoon does not require much thinking. Life is predictable. The safety and security of a closed world is very appealing to some people. The broader world is beyond their comprehension or appreciation and can be mysterious and frightening to them. They do not realize there are legitimate beliefs beyond their way of thinking. They naively believe that their little world is all that exists, or that at least there is nothing of ultimate truth or importance beyond their realm. Sadly, they don't have an appreciation of the fact that there is a whole new world out there that is enjoyed by liberated butterflies.

Some churches want their members to stay in cocoons. They are easier to keep in line. Cocooned parishioners do not ask difficult questions, and they do not venture out on their own. Butterflies, on the other hand, explore freely. Their lives are exciting, fun and rewarding, though uncontrollable and somewhat risky. There is no end to the possibilities in a butterfly's unfettered world for learning and growth.

Jesus used the analogy of wind to describe his followers, those who are born of the Spirit. He said, "The wind blows where it chooses, and you hear the sound of it, but you do not know where it comes from or where it goes" (John 3:8). The wind is unpredictable and beyond our control. Jesus goes on to say, "So it is with everyone who is born of the Spirit" (John 3:8).

Sadly, not only do many people in spiritual stage two fail to grow beyond that stage themselves, but worse, they prevent others from moving on as well. This is not a new phenomenon. Jesus observed it in the scribes and Pharisees, the most staunch stage two people of his day. He told them, "But woe to you scribes, Pharisees, hypocrites! For you lock people out of the kingdom of heaven. For you do not go in yourselves, and when others are going in, you stop them" (Matthew 23:13).

Stage two people often feel threatened and concerned when they witness others moving into stage three, which they see manifested in the expression of honest questions and doubts. Their deep concerns are based on the misinterpretation of where the people growing into stage three are headed. It appears that the others are not progressing spiritually, but have slid back to spiritual stage one. They mistakenly believe that those who are growing have actually lost their faith and abandoned Christ. This conclusion is inevitable for them because, while they are familiar with stages one and two, they have no first hand knowledge of stages three and four. They have not experienced them. Indeed, they are not aware that there are possibilities for growth beyond their present spiritual level. For them, stage two is the model for Christianity and the ultimate standard for the faith. They cannot comprehend how anyone with questions and doubts could be more advanced spiritually than they.

When people grow from stage two to three, often interpreted as backsliding, the immediate response of those remaining in stage two is to try to lasso the people they believe have gone astray and lead them back into the fold. To use another analogy, stage two people often chase after newly liberated butterflies with a net in an attempt to bring them back into the cocoon. Though well intentioned, the end result of these efforts is that they hinder others from progressing into stage three. Without realizing it, they are holding others back in their spiritual growth. Sadly, they prevent many people from ever reaching the ultimate spiritual experience of stage four.

While it is unfortunate to get stuck in stage two, it is not necessarily better to move on to stage three and stop there. Remaining plagued by unresolved questions and doubts is neither enriching nor fulfilling. There is no power in a life of uncertainty.

In light of the above, you can see our goal should be to move through the spiritual stages to stage four. Vitality, power and excitement become realities when our inner confusion and questions are resolved, when spiritual truths come into focus and are ingrained in our lives.

Growth for Eternity

I believe growth is as essential in the next life as it is in our earthly existence; it is just not possible to do all of our growing here. Each of us uses only a small percentage of the mental capacity given us. We are far from developing our full physical potential as well, a fact born out by the many people who continue to set new world records in athletic competition. When I think of the possibilities of depth in our spiritual growth, it is apparent to me that most of us have only begun to grow.

In the Christian faith we celebrate the present reality as well as future expectation. It is wonderful to experience joy, peace, forgiveness, empowerment, love, and so much more. Yet, looking to the future, we can expect fulfillment and happiness far beyond what we can even imagine now. I can hardly wait for what tomorrow will bring.

So growth is necessary, and is possible throughout eternity. It is possible because of the power, love and grace of God. Because God is great, wonderful and powerful, there is no limit to the possibilities for growth. Our ultimate goal is to become as one with God.

The Bible includes some great affirmations about God's people. It begins with creation, according to Genesis 1:26: "Then God said, 'Let us make humankind in our image.'" Later, in Psalms 8:5 we hear, "You have made them a little lower than God, and crowned them with glory and honor." And in 1 Peter 2:9 we read, "But you are a chosen race, a royal priesthood, a holy nation, God's own people." First, the Bible tells us people are very special and, as we study further, we see that there are no limits to what we might one day become. I wonder how many of us believe, like God does, that by God's grace, love and power working through us, our potential is unlimited. I'm convinced God has every intention of ultimately making endless growth a reality for each of us.

So there is the exciting reality of growth in this life and the next. Those who die and go to heaven will not have arrived at their final destination. There will continue to be opportunities for, and the necessity of, learning and growing in one's abilities and relationships with God and others.

No one will ever arrive, nor should it necessarily be considered desirable to do so. To have arrived could be like retiring, our work done, with nothing left to do; no more challenges, or learning, or growth. If that is the case, to have arrived could make heaven seem boring and unfulfilling. If it were ever truly possible to have arrived, wouldn't that also open up the possibility of pride and smugness on the part of those who thought they had arrived (which would only prove that they hadn't)? Heaven would not be completely heavenly if that were possible.

Unending growth naturally implies that we will not only need the grace and forgiveness of God at this time, in this life, but we always will. In our journey as imperfect people who have not arrived, in this life and the next, God helps us to grow, nurtures us along, and forgives our failures and shortcomings all along the way.

One way to express this is to say that God functions as our counselor, now as well as later. The understanding of God as our counselor should come as no surprise to us since the Messiah is referred to as, "Wonderful Counselor, Mighty God" (Isaiah 9:6). In reference to the Holy Spirit, Jesus said that the Father "will give you another Advocate (commonly translated Counselor), to be with you forever" (John 14:16).

Many of us are too proud to willingly seek out a counselor. But if we could get beyond our pride, we might discover the purpose of such a relationship; to help us gain insight into our behavior and ourselves. A counselor is one who holds us accountable for our actions, one that helps us overcome our misconceptions and leads us in a path of growth. Through such a process we might learn to let go of our addictions, fears, prejudices and our need to control others. We might learn to be loving, forgiving, kind, healthy and whole. God's Spirit is our greatest counselor now, along with truly spiritual and insightful people who help guide us in God's ways. I believe that through the Holy Spirit and those gifted individuals God provides, our growth process will continue into eternity.

Heaven offers the possibility, indeed, the necessity of continual, eternal growth as one advances toward the fullness of God. I believe that is what Paul is referring to in 2 Corinthians 12:2, where he writes, "I know a person in Christ who fourteen years ago was caught up in the third heaven." This Scripture suggests there are different levels which one may experience in one's relationship with God and others in heaven, where people "with unveiled faces, seeing the glory of the Lord. . . . are being transformed into the same image from one degree of glory to another" (2 Corinthians 3:18).

One way to understand the different and progressive levels of heaven is to think of them as inns along the road. Some people have interpreted the reference to "many dwelling places" (John 14:2) to pertain to this. So when you die you arrive at the first inn by the side of the road. There you meet your loved ones, and after resting a while you awaken one day to, in Lesley Weatherhead's words, "find that there is a road stretching on beyond you, and that there are more inns at the side of the road. Then you progress into deeper appreciation of human fellowship, but with also a deepening appreciation of divine fellowship, as you move along that road."[3]

I like that concept of heaven. Rather than possessing a mansion in which to live, one is provided many dwelling places as one advances along the road toward the fullness of God, "being transformed into (God's) image from one degree of glory to another."

Chapter Nine

MISERY LOVES COMPANY

Why Some People Cling to the Idea
of Eternal Damnation

God will eventually save everyone. What a thought! What a resounding acclamation! Sadly, though, many people do not believe in it, so they cannot join in the joyful celebration. We can't blame most of them because they have never been told about universal salvation. When they are told, many respond favorably while others are somewhat cautious about accepting the news. Some people, upon hearing of universal salvation, consider it such good news that they latch onto it like a child onto a teddy bear.

Negative Responses to the Good News
In bold contrast to the joyous enthusiasm of many people, others seem determined not to believe that everyone will be saved. Karl Barth seems rather perplexed with that kind of response, when he says it is a "strange Christianity, whose most pressing anxiety seems to be that God's grace might prove to be all too free on this side, that hell, instead of being populated with so many people, might someday prove to be empty!"[1]

It amazes me how some folks cling so tenaciously to the

very unpleasant concept of eternal damnation, rather than to embrace the good news of universal salvation. An announcement that God will eventually save everyone should cause great relief, celebration and dancing in the streets. You would think people (especially Christians, who claim to serve a God of love and compassion) would welcome the idea that no one will have to spend eternity in hell. But that is not always the case.

Some people I have encountered apparently want to continue to believe in the eternal damnation of the unsaved. Why is it so near and dear to their hearts that they are not about to give it up under any circumstance? After wrestling with that question, I have come to realize the first clue is that it is near and dear to their hearts. It is not that the idea of eternal damnation is so special, but that their personal beliefs are fastened to their hearts like the love reserved for the closest of friends. They have received great comfort and security in what they have believed, perhaps for many decades. Changing beliefs after that length of time is like closing the door on their oldest companions.

Also, as I have previously stated, many people are threatened by change. It is frightening to follow truth wherever it leads. Some people are unable or unwilling to attempt it; in their insecurities they cling to the past, to what is familiar, to what seems safe.

We can understand why many people will not accept the hope of universal salvation, but those factors do not explain why some react so strongly against it. I have met some people who become judgmental or downright hostile toward me when I tell them that God will eventually save everyone. I struggled to understand why they reacted that way, until some of the reasons were verbalized to me, and then other more subtle reasons slowly became apparent. These reasons relate to unconscious dynamics that may have a profound influence on what people believe and how they act.

Verbalized Reasons for Opposing Universalism

The most common reason people have given me for rejecting universalism is that they do not believe the Bible supports it. They have often heard the passages which seem to support unending punishment of the unsaved, as I quoted in Chapter One, but they have rarely heard any of those quotations which support universal salvation. This is complicated by the fact that Bible passages are often interpreted in several different ways.

When I have spoken to them of the often overlooked and misunderstood passages, sometimes offering an interpretation different from what their schooling might lead them to expect, they may initially feel unnerved or threatened. They believe I am tampering with the Scriptures. This strikes at the very foundation of their faith and the religion they believe they should never question.

The fact that most people are unaware of the strong biblical support for universalism is not surprising to me. Most people have received the majority of their information in a church setting. Seminaries do not teach ministers that God will eventually save everyone, so ministers naturally do not preach and teach about it in their churches.

Beyond that, some church leaders who do know about universal salvation do not want anyone else to find out about it. It is evident to me that, among these people, there exists what is in effect a conspiracy of silence. Conspiracy by definition is an act by two or more in secret. Consciously or subconsciously, no one speaks about it. The reason they attempt to keep other people uninformed is because church leaders have a vested interest in maintaining the doctrine of eternal damnation. We will explore what church leaders hope to gain from silence in the upcoming discussion on co-dependence.

I have known people who act like the scribes and Pharisees as depicted in the New Testament by begrudging God's generosity in the granting of salvation. Such actions should not be too surprising to any of us. Membership in an exclusive group has a strong appeal for many people. Some people, while contemplating salvation of others, like to think of themselves as an important part of the in-group. They assume from their lofty position that the others are the ones to be left out. The modern day scribes and Pharisees, as has always been the case, derive satisfaction and comfort from the quite unnecessary belief that many will be condemned. They contend, "That sinner got what he deserved." Naturally, they never consider themselves as condemned.

The most strongly expressed motivation for those who oppose universal salvation is fear. They fear that if the fact that God will eventually save everyone becomes widely known, some people (especially their own children or other loved ones) will not take hell seriously. As a result, some of their precious loved ones may be inclined to live in an evil way while they still expect to get into heaven. What if they enter the next life only to learn it doesn't work that way? With that thought in mind, some people, out of genuine concern for the eternal well-being of their loved ones, emphatically reject the idea that God will eventually save everyone. Consequently, they sometimes emotionally berate those who believe God will.

Co-dependence

I believe there often exists an unhealthy co-dependent relationship between the Church and its members. Unfortunately, that co-dependency gives people a psychological reason to cling to the belief in eternal damnation. Co-dependence involves an unhealthy perception of oneself and relating to other people in detrimental ways. There are many characteristics of co-dependency, including; an inability to deal with feelings openly, the need to maintain control over others and situations, the inordinate need to please others, perfectionism, dishonesty, fearfulness, rigidity, judgmentalism, self-centeredness, and negativism.

For example, there is commonly a co-dependent relationship between an alcoholic and his family. The alcoholic depends on his family to cover up his drinking, such as calling an employer with an excuse for his absence from work. The family members are dependent on the alcoholic for physical and psychological support, while often subconsciously wanting the alcoholic to continue to drink so they can maintain a degree of control over him. Typically, everyone in the family is manipulative and tries to control everyone else. Every family member is ultimately motivated by self-preservation and the desire to maintain control of their lives; lives dominated by fear. They hide their true feelings and seek acceptance from others by trying to be perfect. Their drive for perfection inevitably fails and that results in low self-esteem.

Leaders in the field of co-dependency contend that the majority of people are co-dependent to one degree or another. There are many factors contributing to this situation, including the dynamics of relationships in our families, schools, places of employment, and even churches. Co-dependency is pervasive throughout our culture and has a major effect on people's lives, yet many people fail to recognize it. Anne Wilson Schaef states in her book, *Co-Dependency Misunderstood - Mistreated*, that the family, school, and Church "teach us to think what we are told to think, feel what we are told to feel, see what we are told to see, and know what we are told to know."[2]

While we prefer to believe that the Church has only a positive influence on people's lives, I am saddened to realize that is not always the case. It is becoming more and more clear to me that the Church sometimes contributes to this problem of co-dependency by way of an unhealthy use of power and control.

While what I am going to say in the following pages regarding co-dependency within the Church may sound rather negative, I would like for us to keep in mind that good things can and do happen in churches in spite of co-dependence. Co-dependence is just one of many dynamics within churches, most of which are positive. The Church has never been perfect, so reform and revitalization has always been an ongoing need. The Church has nonetheless functioned in a wonderful way over the centuries. God has used the Church powerfully through its strengths, in spite of its weaknesses.

Through the Church, billions of people have been helped to receive salvation by God's grace, and to experience joyful realities such as love, peace, forgiveness and encouragement. Countless worship opportunities have drawn people together for conversion, praise and celebration. People have been motivated and equipped to go forth to share the news of salvation through Christ and to serve others in love. The Church has served magnificently over the years. I, like so many others, love Christ's Church. I am eternally grateful for being saved through Christ, as well as for the ongoing loving influence of the many wonderful church people in my life.

As special as the Church is, however, it is not without blemish or weakness. One of its weaknesses is co-dependency. The co-dependent relationship that often exists between the Church and its members is a significant reason for the perpetuation of the teaching of eternal damnation. Conversely, teaching eternal damnation perpetuates co-dependency. It is a vicious cycle.

Co-dependence Throughout Church History

To understand the cycle of co-dependency within churches, it is helpful to put it into a historical perspective. To a large degree this revolves around the theologian and Church leader Augustine and his teachings. Universal salvation was well accepted and widely believed by Christians until the sixth century. It was then banished due to the influence of Augustine's teachings against it. Thereafter, the teaching of everlasting punishment of the unsaved prevailed in the Church for over 1,000 years, until after the Protestant Reformation. The history of universalism will be addressed in greater length in the next chapter.

The teaching of eternal damnation gave the Church tremendous power and control over its members through the threat of excommunication, which amounted to being cut off from the sacraments and fellowship of the Church. Church leaders could convince their members to believe almost anything (such as, the Pope is infallible) or to do nearly anything (such as, give large sums of money to the Church while leaving themselves in poverty) by threatening to excommunicate them.

The teeth in the threat of excommunication was the perception that the Church was the exclusive dispenser of salvation. People were taught that the Church held the keys to heaven and hell, as according to Matthew 16:19, Jesus said to Peter, "I will give you the keys of the kingdom of heaven, and whatever you bind on earth will be bound in heaven, and whatever you loose on earth will be loosed in heaven." The Church, by this teaching, was perceived to possess the keys to heaven.

The Church also claimed authority to consign a person to hell if he or she did not abide by the Church's mandates. In those days, if a worshipper was expelled from the Church, it was believed that he or she had been given a one-way ticket to hell. With the understanding that a person who went to hell would be confined there forever, church members did not take the Church's threats lightly.

Another way the Church controlled its members was to keep them ignorant of the Scriptures by copying the Bible only in Latin. Virtually no one but priests ever learned Latin, so the common people were completely at the mercy of the priests and church leaders if they were to learn more about their religion. The priests told the people only what they wanted them to know about what the Bible said. While people were taught about eternal damnation for the unsaved, they were told nothing about universal salvation. In other words, the common people were taught the "party line" and threatened with eternal damnation if they did not follow it.

As you can see, in the Church, there existed a very unhealthy co-dependent relationship. The Church exercised total control over its members, while the members allowed themselves to be controlled. They often did not think for themselves, but instead, did what they were told to do in exchange for the promise of salvation.

This extreme situation continued until the time of the

Protestant Reformation, which began under the leadership of Martin Luther in the year 1517. With the formation of other churches, the Roman Catholic Church no longer held exclusive power. The threat of excommunication was no longer as dire a circumstance because, if excommunicated, a person could join another church, although the Roman Catholics still maintained that they were the only true church. Leaving the Roman Catholic Church to join another church, however, would have been like jumping out of the frying pan into the fire. All churches taught the eternal damnation of the unsaved. None were willing to give up that foolproof way to control their members. Also, collectively, the churches of the day still considered themselves the exclusive conduit of God's grace and salvation.

The invention of the printing press was probably the most significant development that made the Protestant Reformation possible. Because of its use, Bibles and other literature could be produced in large quantities. People no longer had to simply accept the teachings of those few who could read and interpret Bibles written in Latin. In the latter half of the fifteenth century and in the early part of the sixteenth century, Bibles became available in the languages of the people (French, Spanish, Italian, Bohemian, German and English) and were mass produced.[3] Consequently, the Church could no longer control the people by keeping them ignorant of what the Scriptures really taught.

Even after personal Bibles were made available, however, people were seldom encouraged to interpret the Scriptures for themselves. While common folk became more enlightened (such as the realization that salvation comes through faith by grace, rather than through good works, rituals, or financial contributions), ministers and church leaders still told the people what to consider as the correct interpretation of the Bible.

This so called correct interpretation of the Bible did not include the teaching of salvation for everyone, but emphasized eternal damnation of the unsaved. The clergy and church leaders, eager to hang on to their means of controlling people, instilled in them fear of eternal damnation. In their conspiracy of silence regarding universal salvation, it seems they hoped no one would discover the passages of Scripture that support it. But that was not possible. People began to read the Bible and to think for themselves. They discovered those overlooked and misunderstood passages and some of them started to believe, like so many Christians in the early Church, that God will eventually save everyone. By the eighteenth century, universalism once again became a strong movement; many people came to believe in it. Still they very rarely received any official endorsement of their belief by the churches.

Co-dependence Today

Co-dependence remains a powerful force in some churches up to the present day. Many people are still told, to a lesser or greater extent, what they must believe, depending on the denomination to which they belong. The official position of nearly all churches continues to uphold the belief in the eternal punishment in hell of the unsaved. Those who voice a different view often receive stern warnings about their impending doom. There is a resounding silence emanating from seminaries and from churches with regard to the question of universal salvation. Apparently the Church still hopes that people will not discover this concept of hope on their own. Also, to the present day, many Christians consider the organized Church as the official and exclusive dispenser of salvation.

An illustration from the church of which I am a member indicates that the Church still believes it is the exclusive conduit for salvation. This illustration can be found in the introduction to one of the baptismal services in *The United Methodist Hymnal*. It reads as follows: "The Church is of God, and will be preserved to the end of time, for. . .the conversion of the world. All, of every age and station, stand in need of the means of grace which it alone supplies."[4]

Another example of the exclusive conduit for salvation doctrine espoused by churches in general is that the Church often gives clergy at the time of their ordination exclusive authority to baptize and serve Holy Communion. I have always personally felt uncomfortable with that concept, as if through my having been ordained I had been given some kind of magical and exclusive power. I do not believe it is the minister, but the presence and working of God's Spirit, which makes sacraments special. Maintaining this exclusive role for the clergy can be the Church's means of controlling people by making them believe that the Church is indispensable for providing salvation by serving as a mediator between themselves and God.

As you can see, we often still have a co-dependent relationship between the Church and its members. Granted, it is not as extreme or unhealthy in most cases as it sometimes was in the past, but co-dependency is still very much a reality. An integral part of this continuing disservice to humanity remains the teaching of eternal damnation of the unsaved.

In order to be fair to the many different denominations and individual churches, I need to make it clear that there are many differences between churches. Some have very little co-dependence, while others are extremely co-dependent. Most fall somewhere in between.

In churches that have a low level of co-dependency, people are not taught a rigid set of beliefs, but are encouraged to think for themselves. Fear is not used against members as a means to control them. The benefits of serving God are emphasized rather than the consequences of an unfaithful life. God is portrayed as loving and forgiving, not angry and judgmental.

In contrast to the churches with low co-dependency, there are others with very high levels. They can be identified by their insistence that all of their members adhere to certain specific beliefs. Members observe each other for infractions of the rules. Thinking for oneself is strongly discouraged. Hell-fire and brimstone sermons are common. A strong sense of urgency is pressed upon the members to get themselves saved before they die; they must avoid going to hell forever. After all, they believe God is very demanding and won't hesitate to send them there. They often quote this Bible passage; "I never knew you;

go away from me, you evil-doers" (Matthew 7:23). They not only teach that the Church in general is indispensable, but often contend that their specific church is the only true way to God, salvation and heaven.

The level of co-dependence in a given church is in direct proportion to the strength of its emphasis on the importance of adhering to a rigid set of beliefs, the eternal damnation of the unsaved, and the teaching that the Church (especially their church) is indispensable for providing salvation.

Chapter Eight outlined the four stages of spiritual growth, and it is my belief that most churchgoers are in stage two of their spiritual development. It should not surprise us that most church people fit into that stage. They are those who fit quite comfortably into the co-dependent relationship that exists between the Church and its members. They look to the Church for structure, governance (control), and guidance on how to live their lives. While they believe that God is a loving being, they tend to think of God as one who does not hesitate to punish sinners (the unsaved).

We also should not be surprised to discover that people experiencing stage two in their spiritual development are those who get the most upset with and judgmental of others who espouse the teaching of universal salvation. The tenets of universalism strike at much of what has become sacred and dear to them, and it exposes their co-dependence. That is a frightening discovery. The more co-dependent a person is, the more he or she is threatened by the concept of universal salvation.

Co-dependency within the Church is a very enticing trap. In its most extreme form, the gains for the leaders and for the Church in general are obvious; the power, control, and authority over members who give generous donations while they volunteer their time to keep the Church operating. What the members get out of this arrangement is the promise of salvation. This is in exchange for not thinking for themselves, while they believe and do what they are told.

There is also another dimension to what the members

receive. As saved members of the Church, and a part of the in-group, they can feel something of that same sense of power and control that is exerted over them. As a result, they often make pronouncements regarding who is saved or lost. They perceive that they speak on behalf of God.

Sadly, this co-dependent relationship is not likely to end soon, nor is the teaching of eternal damnation. These two factors are bound together and perpetuate one another. Without the teaching of eternal damnation, the Church would lose its ability to manipulate and control.

When we believe that God will eventually save everyone, including saving people from hell, we are forced to realize and admit that we do not have control. God does! Isn't it just like God to be out of control (Out of our control, that is)? Many people tend to not like a God such as that. They prefer to believe that they are in control, that they have the grace (to dole out or withhold), that they have the keys (to open heaven or lock hell). And they delude themselves into believing that God agrees with them.

Before leaving this subject, I need to state that dependence in relationships is not bad in and of itself. Far from it! It can be very healthy to depend on others in various ways. Children depend on their parents for guidance as well as to satisfy their many physical and emotional needs. We all depend on friends for support, encouragement and help. We depend on our loved ones to stand by us when times are hard, and to celebrate with us in good times. Mutually dependent and supportive relationships help us to learn and grow, to become all God wants us to be, to enable us to relate to God and others in such a way that we experience heaven in this life and beyond. Ultimately, we depend upon God for salvation, who by grace gives it to us as a free gift. Dependence can be, and often is, wonderfully positive. It is important that the Church be about nurturing those kinds of positive relationships.

Sadly, however, we need to be aware that dependence in relationships sometimes slips into co-dependence, which can be very destructive. Instead of encouragement, there is control.

Instead of hope, there is fear. Instead of support, there is judgment. Instead of forgiveness, there is the expectation of perfection. Instead of openness, there is dishonesty. Co-dependence can produce profoundly negative consequences in the way people relate to each other, including in the Church.

God, heal us of our co-dependence and make us whole. Amen!

Chapter Ten

THE ANCIENTS HAVE STOLEN OUR BEST IDEAS

The History Of Universalism

Since it was widely believed in the early centuries of the Christian Church that God would eventually save everyone, most Christians of the time did not consider universal salvation a radical idea. Those who believed in it were not thought of as heretics.

As time passed though, the situation changed. Strong opposition to Universalism developed in the fifth and sixth centuries and steps were taken to abolish its teaching. Because of the threat of banishment and persecution of its adherents after that time, the belief largely died out and lay dormant for many centuries. Since the eighteenth century, however, many people have once again come to believe in salvation for all, although not without controversy.

The Early Church

The doctrine of endless punishment in hell for the unsaved was widely believed by pagans and heathens (any religion other than the Jewish or Christian faiths, such as the religions of the Greeks, Romans or Africans, all of which were referred to by the Jews as, "Gentiles") before the time of Christ and into the early years of the Church. The Jews also believed it. When people of those religions were converted to Christianity they sometimes retained their belief of unending punishment of the wicked. In that setting, it was often difficult to convince people that the wicked would not be punished eternally. So it is of great significance that "the Christian writers employed *aionios*, meaning indefinite but limited duration, and *kotasin*, denoting chastisement resulting in reformation, to describe the nature and duration of punishment, while the Jews and pagans used *aidios* and *adialeiptos* meaning eternal, and *eirgmos*, imprisonment, and *timoria*, torment. Our Lord and his apostles carefully abstained from expressing or implying the popular error by never using the terms employed by those of their contemporaries who taught it."[1]

During the time of the early Church, Christians thought about the fate of the unsaved from three different perspectives. Some taught that after death the unsaved would merely be annihilated. Others believed that they would experience endless punishment in the hereafter. Still others taught that God would eventually save everyone.[2]

The first Christian theological school was founded in Alexandria in the second century. The first scholar of note connected with that school was Anaxagoras, followed by Pantaenus,[3] then by Clement in 189 A.D.,[4] and Origen in 203 A.D.[5] For all of these theological leaders, Greek was their mother tongue. Thus, they would have known very well the meaning of the words of the language in which the New Testament was written. That would not have been true of many people who came later, such as Augustine, who never mastered Greek.

Both Clement and Origen believed very strongly that God would eventually save everyone. "Clement would not tolerate the thought that any soul would continue forever to resist the force of redeeming love. Somehow and somewhere in the long run of ages that love must prove weightier than sin and death, and vindicate its power in one universal triumph."[6] Origen, who was born of Christian parents in 186 A.D.,[7] wrote in his book, *On First Principles*, "There is a resurrection of the dead, and there is punishment but not everlasting. For when the body is punished the soul is gradually purified."[8]

Tertullian, a man of heathen parentage who became a Christian when he was about 40 years old and was a contemporary of Origen, believed in the everlasting punishment of the wicked.[9] Tertullian took things to the extreme with his teachings regarding the wicked being punished in hell. In fact, he believed, according to what he wrote in his treatise, *On Spectacles*, that the best thing about heaven was "its superb view of the damned frying in hell."[10] Not surprisingly, Origen thought Tertullian's belief was outrageous and abhorrent. He found it diametrically opposed to his own thinking that all punishments in this world and the next are remedial, and that they are a part of God's plan to bring all people home to God.

During that time, universal salvation was taught not only in Alexandria, but in three other theological schools as well. They were at Caesarea, Antioch and Edessa. The schools at Alexandria and Caesarea followed Clement and Origen, while the ones at Antioch and Edessa were led by Theodore of Mopsuestia and Diodore of Tarsus.[11]

There are many indications that universal salvation was widely accepted in the early Church. It was commonly taught that Christ had preached the Gospel to the dead in Hades, and many contended that all of the damned were released. Prayers for the release of the dead from hell were very common, which would have been foolishness if people believed that their fate had been irretrievably fixed at the time of death.[12] Works refuting all the known heresies of the times were written by Irenaeus (120-202 A.D.) and Hippolytus (170-235 A.D.). Universal salvation was not listed among the heresies.[13]

Universalism was still a very strong belief in the fourth century,[14] when the theologian and bishop, Gregory of Nyssa (c. 335-394)[15] forcefully taught that God would eventually save everyone. He believed evil was merely the corruption or disfigurement of that which was good. Evil, therefore, had no substance in its own right, and had to eventually come to an end, in contrast to good, which would endure forever since it is genuine substance. Gregory of Nyssa rejected the idea of everlasting punishment because such punishment could only be considered vindictive. He believed that God did not punish in a vindictive sense but only for the purpose of drawing people into communion with God. Punishment, according to him, was merely the painful side of people's journey back to God, and everyone would eventually complete that journey.[16]

Aside from Augustine, the two most influential people in the Church during the second half of the fourth century were Ambrose and Jerome.[17] They both believed in universal salvation. Ambrose (c. 334-397)[18] a church leader and the Bishop of Milan, taught that the salvation of one of the criminals who was crucified with Jesus proves that no one can be excluded from the forgiveness of God. He said that while people are merciful toward their neighbors, God's mercy extends to all people, so all will be saved.[19]

Jerome (c.340-420), whose Latin translation of the Bible, the *Vulgate*, is still in use in the Roman Catholic Church,[20] was an especially strong advocate of universalism early in his ministry. He "took Origen as his model and inspiration during his early years. . . . His early *Commentary on Ephesians*, for instance, which apparently draws on Origen *verbatim* in many passages, confidently predicts that 'all rational creatures' will 'see the glory of God in ages to come'; each will be restored to its original place and role in God's creation, even the 'renegade angels.'"[21]

Augustine

Augustine's (354-430 A.D.) father was a heathen and his mother, a Christian. Augustine was converted to Christianity at the age of 32. He soon became a very strong leader in the Church.[22] Consistent with his heathen roots, Augustine believed in the endless punishment of the wicked.

He did not believe, however, that everyone who died without being saved was necessarily destined for an eternity in hell. He believed that some of the dead, who are condemned to be punished after death because of their sins, would eventually be released from punishment. That would take place because of being purged of their sinfulness by their own suffering or because of the prayers of other Christians.[23] The reason he could teach both endless punishment of the wicked and salvation for some who weren't saved before death is because he made a very clear distinction "between time--to which even the dead still belong--and eternity."[24] According to Augustine, eternity doesn't begin until after the resurrection and the final judgment. Until that time, whether people are alive or dead, there is the possibility of conversion.

"Augustine frequently insists, however, that not all the dead are capable of receiving God's mercy through the prayers and meritorious actions of the Church done in their name."[25] Those people, after the resurrection of the body, experience the final judgment of God and are sent to hell, the second death, to stay there forever. On the other hand, those who have passed from death to life will escape the second death and go to heaven.[26]

Once people have gone into eternity and are suffering in hell, "Augustine's understanding of punishment is, in fact, wholly vindictive: God's truth and justice require that the creature who turns away from him, the one authentic source of its being, should suffer as a result."[27] Then, according to Augustine, it will be too late to repent and that will contribute to the anguish experienced in hell, as they will "be tortured by fruitless repentance."[28]

Augustine believed that the suffering of the people in hell will be extreme, teaching that "the doom in store for those who are not in the City of God is an unending wretchedness. . . . pounded by perpetual pain. . . . the punishment must never end."[29] He strongly challenged those who believed that the pain would end, and that all people would eventually be saved. He wrote, "Now I must. . .deal. . .with some of our own tenderhearted fellow Christians, who are inclined to feel that there must sooner or later be liberation from hell. . .that happiness will be eternal for all who, sooner or later, are freed from torments. . . . But the fact is that the more merciful the theory is, the more it contradicts the words of God and, therefore, the further it is from the truth."[30] The fact that Augustine addressed the issue of universal salvation and spoke so forcefully against it is an indication of just how strong the movement was at that time.

Augustine was willing to make a bit of a concession, however, to those who argued that God's mercy extends even to the most hardened sinners. He contended that, even though God is merciful, that "should not be taken to mean that the wicked will be wholly exempt from the pains or that the pains will finally come to an end. The most that can be said is that the pains suffered may be lighter and milder than the wickedness has deserved."[31]

Opposition and Condemnation of Universalism

Augustine, who was a great theologian in many respects, developed a significant following and his theology soon became dominant in the Church. Largely due to his influence, there came to be increasing opposition to the doctrine of universal salvation. Brian Daley presents a detailed account of that controversy.[32] He writes that Origen's Theology, including his teaching that everyone would eventually be saved, had been somewhat controversial even before the sixth century, but the debate over it became particularly bitter during the second quarter of that century.

The Emperor Justinian ruled the Roman Empire from 527 to 565 A.D. During his reign, church leaders who opposed Origen's teachings sought his help and support in stopping the spread of the belief that God would eventually save everyone. In 543 Justinian issued an Imperial Edict in which he attacked Origen and his teachings, including those regarding the limited duration of all punishment. He included and discussed the edict in a letter to the patriarch Menas (or Mennos) of Constantinople. He claimed that Origen's teachings made people lazy about keeping God's commandments.[33]

Over the centuries the leaders of the Christian Church have gathered from time to time for ecumenical councils to address major issues facing the Church. Justinian convened the Fifth Ecumenical Council at Constantinople in the spring of 553. One of the subjects they addressed was Origen's theology. That Ecumenical Council issued 15 statements condemning the teachings of Origen. After the Ecumenical Council's condemnation of Origenist Theology, some of Origen's teachings, including his position on universal salvation, were considered heresy throughout the Church.

The meaning of the Greek word *aionios* was central to the issue of Origen's theology, because it relates to the length of punishment in hell. Origen believed *aionios* meant, "indefinite but limited duration" (as I've noted in Chapter One), so when the Bible makes reference to eternal (*aionios*) punishment, he believed that meant the punishment would eventually come to an end. That understanding of *aionios* was basic to his belief in universal salvation.

John Wesley Hanson informs us that Augustine "was the first known to argue that *aionios* signified endless. He at first maintained that it always meant thus, but at length abandoned that ground, and only claimed that it had that meaning sometimes."[34]

It is of great significance that Justinian did not challenge Origen's understanding of the Greek word *aionios* in his edict of 543. In writing to Menas (or Mennos), Patriarch of Constantinople, about his edict, Justinian found it necessary to add another word in order to support his position. Writing in Greek he says, "The holy church of Christ teaches an endless *aionios* (*ATELEUTETOS aionios*) life to the righteous and endless (*ateleutetos*) punishment to the wicked."[35] In his own words and by his own judgment, the use of the word *aionios* by itself was not sufficient to denote endless duration, so he added to it the word *ateleutetos*. John Wesley Hanson writes, "This demonstrates that even as late as A.D. 540 *aionios* meant limited duration, and required an added word to impart to it the force of endless duration."[36]

Ultimately, we can see Justinian was not able to refute Origen's belief that *aionios* meant limited duration. But because of the influence of Augustine, many people had come to vehemently oppose the teaching of universal salvation. Under strong pressure from that faction, Justinian felt compelled to issue an edict condemning universalism.

To make his edict effective, Justinian went so far as to order that thereafter no bishop or abbot should be ordained unless he condemned universalism. Any bishop or abbot who refused to do so was to be deposed and banished. Following Justinian's edict, the belief in universalism was of necessity kept secret by its adherents. With all the forces of the Church and State against it, the teaching that God will eventually save everyone naturally declined in popularity. After a period of time it virtually died out.[37]

Does it seem strange to you that the Roman Emperor, Justinian, became so involved in the concerns of the Church? This will make complete sense when you see it in the context of co-dependence, where the control of others and situations is a major dynamic. By the sixth century the Roman emperor exerted a great deal of influence over the Church. That was a dramatic change when compared to the situation prior to the early part of the fourth century. At that time, Emperor Constantine declared Christianity an officially accepted and favored religion of the empire. Before Constantine had granted that supposed favor, the Church was a completely independent entity and did not support the State. After Constantine's declaration, a co-dependent relationship quickly developed between the Church and the State. In exchange for acceptance and the elimination of persecution, the Church allowed the State to have a significant amount of influence and control over it. Also, the Church began the practice of giving largely unquestioned support of the State and its conquests and policies.

Before the fourth century most Christians were pacifists who refused to serve in the emperor's armed forces. After Constantine's acceptance of Christianity, Christians began to waiver from their pacifist principles. Rather than to love their enemies as Jesus commanded them according to Matthew 5:43-44, they began to rationalize that it was all right to kill. Once they had convinced themselves it was acceptable to God to hate and destroy enemies, it was a short step for many of them to also believe that God would punish sinners forever. Conversely, those who already believed in unending punishment, with the corresponding violent perception of God, had few serious qualms about serving in the emperor's army.

After more than 200 years of the militarization of the Church and its related eroding effects on Universalist teachings, Justinian became the emperor. Justinian was motivated more by politics than by religious convictions. When the controversy over universal salvation arose it was natural for him to side with those who opposed universalism. They were the ones who were most supportive of him, and the ones he could most easily control. The free spirited Universalists were not easily controlled and thus were considered a threat to others in the Church as well as to the emperor.

It is not surprising; therefore, that Justinian and those who opposed universalism joined forces. They outlawed Universalist teachings and reinforced the doctrine of eternal damnation as a means of attempting to bring everyone under control. This also had the effect of perpetuating the co-dependent relationship between the Church and the State.

John Wesley

The doctrine of universal salvation lay largely dormant for several centuries. Eventually it started to revive, and became quite strong again by the eighteenth century. That was when John Wesley (1703-1791) came on the scene. He was one of the founders of the Methodist movement and had a close association with the Moravians, a body of dedicated Christians who believed in universal salvation. They had a significant influence on him. From early in his ministry, Wesley's teachings held much in common with those who taught that God would eventually save everyone. He preached a sermon entitled, "Salvation By Faith," on June 18, 1738, in which he stated, "this is that great salvation foretold by the angel, before God brought His First-begotten into the world: 'Thou shalt call His name Jesus; for He shall save His people from their sins.' And neither here, nor in other parts of the holy writ, is there any limitation or restriction."[38]

At that time, however, Wesley did not embrace universalism. Instead, in his journal of September 1741, Wesley quotes a Moravian publication that said, "By this His name all can and shall obtain life and salvation,"[39] indicating he didn't agree. He referred to universal salvation and other Moravian teachings as "grand errors."[40]

John Wesley, however, was always a seeker after the truth. Later in his life, his beliefs had evolved to the point where he endorsed universalism. That is illustrated by a sermon that he preached on March 13, 1782, entitled, "On The Fall of Man," in which he said that God loves everyone and God's mercy extends to all. He further contended that it is impossible for the Creator to despise the work of his own hands. God, who alone is able to do it, has provided a remedy for all the evils of humankind. The sufficient remedy for all our guilt is that Christ bore all our sins on the cross. God in his mercy has provided "an universal remedy for an universal evil! In appointing the Second Adam to die for all who had died in the first: that 'as in Adam all died, so in Christ all might be made alive;' that 'as by one man's offense judgment came upon all men to condemnation, so by the righteousness of one' the free gift 'might come upon all, unto justification of life.'"[41]

The American Colonies

The American colonies proved to be the most fertile ground for the spread of the teaching of universalism in the eighteenth century. Dr. George DeBenneville, of French Huguenot background, migrated to Pennsylvania in 1741. He was instrumental in the spreading of Universalist views. John Murray (1741-1815), though, who came from England in 1770, is considered the father of organized Universalism.[42]

While Murray was very actively involved in church work in England, he didn't preach on a regular basis until after he came to America. Upon his arrival, both Quaker and German Baptists who openly taught universalism befriended Murray. Many of the early Universalists in the American colonies were from the Baptist churches.[43] With their encouragement he began to preach regularly,[44] and he had significant success in spreading universalism even though there was much opposition.[45] The Universalists, under Murray's leadership, organized their own church on January 1, 1779.[46]

Hosea Ballou (1771-1852) was a dominant figure in the Universalist Church during his lifetime. "He taught that Christ's sacrificial death was not intended to serve as a pacification of an angry God, but rather serves as a demonstration of God's love for mankind."[47] He wrote, "We now see clearly that it is God's will, according to his eternal purpose, purposed in himself, that all men should finally be holy and happy; that it was the intention of the Savior's mission."[48] By the time of Ballou's death in 1852 there were more than 800,000 adherents to the Universalist faith.[49] The Universalist Church of America merged with the American Unitarian Association in 1961 to become the Unitarian Universalist Association.[50]

Feodor Dostoevsky

The great nineteenth century Russian writer, Feodor Dostoevsky, included a great deal of theology in his works. He strongly believed in universal salvation. He contended that Christ could forgive anyone of anything because his blood was shed for all. He believed that if God couldn't save even the worst of sinners that would mean that God was a failure. But it is not possible for God to fail.[51] What makes Dostoevsky's witness even more powerful is that he wrote of universal salvation at a time when many in Russia denounced the power of God.

Friedrich Schleiermacher

Friedrich Schleiermacher, nineteenth century German Theologian, says there is some of Jesus' sayings that seem to support the conclusion that those who die without having a saving relationship with Christ are doomed to experience the misery of hell forever. He goes on to say that if these sayings are more closely scrutinized, however, they will "be found insufficient to support any such conclusion. . . . Through the power of redemption there will one day be a universal restoration of all souls."[52]

Dietrich Bonhoeffer

Dietrich Bonhoeffer (German theologian and church leader who was put to death in a concentration camp during World War II because of his opposition to the Nazis) believed that the central message of the New Testament is that God reconciled the world with Godself through Christ. He wrote that "the world is not divided between Christ and the devil, but whether it recognizes it or not, it is solely and entirely the world of Christ. . . . There is no part of the world, be it never so forlorn and never so godless, which is not accepted by God and reconciled with God in Jesus Christ."[53]

Karl Barth

Renowned twentieth century Swiss theologian, Karl Barth wrote, "The witness of the community of God to every individual man consists in this: that this choice (rejecting God) of the godless man is void; that he belongs eternally to Jesus Christ and therefore is not rejected, but elected by God in Jesus Christ; that the rejection which he deserves on account of his perverse choice is borne and cancelled by Jesus Christ; that he is appointed to eternal life with God on the basis of the righteous, divine decision."[54]

Paul Tillich

In answer to the question, "who shall be saved, liberated,

healed?" the German-born twentieth century American theologian, Paul Tillich writes, "The fourth gospel says: the world! The reunion with the eternal from which we come, from which we are separated, to which we shall return, is promised to everything that is."[55] Regarding "the eternal destiny of the individual either as being everlastingly condemned or as being everlastingly saved," Tillich goes on to say that brings up the issue of double predestination.

Predestination means that God ordained or determined from eternity what must take place, including fixing each person's destiny for happiness or misery. So, to believe in double predestination is to believe that God arbitrarily decided before the beginning of time which people will go to heaven and which will go to hell for eternity.

The idea that God predestined some people for everlasting hell even before creating them is in direct contrast to the belief that God created everything, including humans, to be perfect and in harmony with God. Genesis 1:31 tells us that, after completing the work of creation, "God saw everything that he had made, and indeed, it was very good."

Tillich says that the issue of double predestination has demonic implications because that suggests there is an eternal split in God. But even without predestination, when you consider the nature of God as well as humans, he believed that one could not defend the conclusion that some people would be in hell forever. Regarding human nature no one is either all bad or all good. "Even the saint remains a sinner and needs forgiveness and even the sinner is a saint in so far as he stands under divine forgiveness. . . . The doctrine of the ambiguity of all human goodness and of the dependence of salvation on the divine grace alone either leads us back to the doctrine of double predestination or leads us forward to the doctrine of universal essentialization."[56]

A Long Rich History

As we can clearly see, the belief in universal salvation is not a recent development. It is not a modern liberal idea, as some might suggest. Universalism has a long rich history. Christians throughout much of the history of the Church have advocated it, especially during the first six centuries and in the last three. The proponents have not always agreed on all points, such as whether or not there will even be hell in the next life, but millions of Christians over time have come to strongly believe and enthusiastically celebrate that God will eventually save everyone.

Chapter Eleven

MAKING MOUNTAINS
OUT OF MOUNTAINS

The Significance Of This Issue

The eternal hell idea is not merely a harmless untruth, about which we can appropriately keep quiet. We may be tempted to not oppose it to avoid the risk of rejection or condemnation from others. But we must speak out against it.

Neither is universal salvation an idea we should keep to ourselves. The importance of sharing the good news of salvation for everyone cannot be overstated. The doctrine of hell has had such an exaggerated place in theology and preaching for so long that for many Christians the good news of the gospel has been overshadowed by the bad news about judgment and punishment. This has gone on far too long, and with devastating consequences.

Atheism

The belief that God sends people to hell to stay there forever is one overwhelming reason many people turn away from God, often to become atheists. That, in turn, adversely affects their behavior and causes them to experience hell. This motivation for turning away from a God of eternal damnation is expressed very well by Samuel Clemens (AKA Mark Twain), where he writes of

> a God who could make good children as easily as bad, yet preferred to make bad ones; who could have made every one of them happy, yet never made a single happy one; who made them prize their bitter life, yet stingily cut it short; who gave his angels eternal happiness unearned, yet required his other children to earn it; who gave his angels painless lives, yet cursed his other children with biting miseries and maladies of mind and body; who mouths justice and invented hell - mouths mercy and invented hell - mouths Golden Rules, and forgiveness multiplied by seventy times seven, and invented hell; who mouths morals to other people and has none himself; who frowns upon crimes, yet commits them all; who created man without invitation, then tries to shuffle the responsibility for man's acts upon man, instead of honorably placing it where it belongs, upon himself; and finally, with altogether divine obtuseness, invites this poor, abused slave to worship him![1]

Not everyone is able to express this as articulately as Twain, but many people feel that way. And they reject God. A strong case can be made that a major reason for atheism is the teaching of a God of eternal damnation.

Mark Twain, as is true of millions of people, was the victim of the teaching of eternal damnation. He wrote, "I cannot see how eternal punishment hereafter could accomplish any good end, therefore I am not able to believe in it. To chasten a man in order to perfect him might be reasonable enough. . .but to roast him forever for the mere satisfaction of seeing him roast would not be reasonable--even the atrocious God imagined by the Jews would tire of the spectacle eventually."[2] Twain could not accept the idea of everlasting punishment. Sadly, however, he threw the baby out with the dirty bath water. He rejected God as well. That caused him to experience a hell of meaninglessness.

Robert Short declares: "Modern atheistic humanism was born out of the inhumaneness of the Monster God. If God is no more humane than this, it was reasoned, then we humans will depend only on ourselves for the foundation of humaneness in the world."[3] According to Twain, "The pulpit says God's ways are not our ways. Thanks. Let us try to get along with our own the best we can; we can't improve on them by experimenting with His."[4]

Bertrand Russell, the author of a book entitled, *Why I am not a Christian,* makes it clear that he rejected the Christian faith because of the teaching of everlasting punishment of the unsaved. He had the impression that Jesus believed in punishment without end, which he considered a serious defect in Christ's moral character. Believing that no really humane person could believe in everlasting punishment, he wrote, "I must say that I think all this doctrine, that hell-fire is a punishment for sin, is a doctrine of cruelty. It is a doctrine that put cruelty into the world and gave the world generations of cruel torture."[5]

Russell was also deeply bothered by what, according to some Christians, determines whether a person experiences endless bliss or endless woe in the next life. He states; "For example, if you died immediately after a priest had sprinkled water upon you while pronouncing certain words, you inherited eternal bliss; whereas, if after a long and virtuous life you happened to be struck by lightning at a moment when you were using bad language because you had broken a bootlace, you would inherit eternal torment."[6]

Ruth Hurmence Green, a member of the Freedom From Religion Foundation, is the author of a book, entitled, *The Born Again Skeptic's Guide to the Bible.* She proclaims, "I'm fond of saying that reading the Bible turned me into an atheist."[7] It is obvious from her book that a major reason for her becoming an atheist and wanting freedom from religion is because of the teaching of a God of eternal damnation. She claims that the Lord of the Old Testament is pretty despicable, but probably not any worse than the Father of the New. That is because the wrath of the Old Testament God was swift and direct, and "didn't await some indeterminate date, in preparation for which the Christian God stokes the coals of hell, anticipating the pleasure of inflicting 'deserved' punishment. . . . What human father would subject his children to a proving ground, where their relationship with him would be the criterion which would determine that most of them would be found wanting, and for this failure be sentenced to eternal agony in a place the father had fashioned ahead of time?"[8] She says that no human parent could be as depraved as that, and with that understanding, God would surely not be considered the author of love and compassion. Because of this perception of God and hell, she rejects God. Many others have done the same.

Communism

According to Robert Short, the development of modern Fascism and Communism was inevitable because of the teaching of endless punishment in hell.[9] Ponder for a moment the implications of this. It is tragic when one person becomes an atheist. It is a tragedy of monumental proportions when atheism becomes institutionalized, as has been the case in the countries of the Soviet Union, China, Cuba and others. While I know that there are many complex reasons for what happens within nations, I believe those countries would have been much less likely to become officially atheistic if God had been consistently presented in a more favorable and accurate way.

Now, Communism is crumbling, which is inevitable with atheism, and the Church is leading the way in overcoming it. But this time, may the Church abandon its teachings on the God of eternal damnation and thus prevent a resurgence of atheism in the future.

Pessimism

Ultimately it is very difficult, perhaps impossible, to be anything but a pessimist, for one who is an atheist. Kurt Vonnegut, author of *Wampeters, Foma & Granfalloons* and many other books, has attested to that. In a commencement address, he said he used to be an optimist. When he was young, his brother helped him to become very enthusiastic about science. He thought science was the answer to the world's problems, that scientific truth was going to make everyone happy and comfortable, but it did not work out that way. What happened instead was that scientific knowledge was used to kill millions of people in war.

During World War II, Vonnegut had been a prisoner of war at Dresden. As it was becoming known just how ghastly the German extermination camps had been, he told how he had a heart-to-heart talk with himself. "'Hey, Corporal Vonnegut,' I said to myself, 'maybe you were wrong to be an optimist. Maybe pessimism is the thing.'"[10] He went on to say, "there *is* no light. Everything is going to become unimaginably worse, and never get better again."[11]

Granted, Vonnegut went through hell in war and that kind of destruction and inhumaneness is bound to breed pessimism, but it seems to me that only an atheist could be as pessimistic as he became. Without a doubt, atheism is a dead end road many people are driven to taking because of the teaching of eternal damnation.

Satanism

Certainly one of the most significant and tragic consequences of the teaching of eternal damnation is the rise of Satanism. Not surprisingly, Satanists have a pretty negative view of Christianity and the teaching of eternal damnation, as is indicated in *The Satanic Bible*. They believe that Satan has been a good friend to the Christian Church because he has kept it in business for all these years. Their understanding is that "The Protestant Hell and the Catholic Hell are places of eternal punishment. . .a horrible place of fire and torment."[12]

Satan's worshippers claim that Christians have a false understanding of hell and the devil. They further contend that this has allowed the Christian Church to flourish because it has given Christians an enemy and a basis for threatening others to keep them in line. Satanists depict Christians as saying, "If you give in to the temptation of the devil, you will surely suffer eternal damnation and roast in Hell."[13]

Sometimes we have been told that there is the possibility of being led astray by the devil, even to the extent of selling one's soul to the devil. In response to that, Satanists claim Christians came up with this threat to keep people from straying away from the church, contending that "with scolding fingers and trembling voices, they taught their followers that if they gave in to the temptations of Satan. . .they would have to pay for their sinful pleasures by giving their souls to Satan and suffering in Hell for all eternity."[14]

In the end, Satanists "tell themselves 'This is for me-- why should I continue with a religion which condemns me for everything I do, even though there is nothing actually wrong with it?'"[15] And they declare, "We are no longer supplicating weaklings trembling before an unmerciful 'God' who cares not whether we live or die. We are self-respecting, prideful people--we are Satanists!"[16]

Lukewarm Christianity

A major concern in all churches is inactive members or lukewarm Christians. Teaching of a God of eternal damnation contributes to this situation. Traditionally, the teaching of the Church has gone something like this: God is loving, kind, gracious and forgiving. God sent Jesus to be our Savior. Isn't it wonderful! But incidentally, if you do not accept Jesus as your Savior before you die or do not measure up to God's standards, God will throw you into hell and toss away the key.

Such a schizophrenic God can never have very much success in winning friends and influencing people. It seems to me that many people are drawn to the Church and stay in church for the purpose of getting saved, but they cannot bring themselves to be very enthusiastic about serving such a God. This is surely one reason why many people go to church on only Christmas and Easter. On those occasions, there is no gloom and doom expressed and the Good News is celebrated.

There is no telling how many millions of people this has

affected over the years. Abraham Lincoln, for example, was someone who never became very involved in church, but not because he didn't believe in God. On the contrary, he had a deep faith and a strong commitment to serve God. He, however, was a biblical Christian who believed in Christ's salvation for all people. His proverbial honesty would not allow him to join a church because all of the churches, of which he was aware, taught eternal damnation instead of universal salvation.[17]

Lukewarmness among Christians is generated by the perception that God is schizophrenic. In contrast, when we realize that God ultimately saves everyone, it is natural for us to respond with unreserved love, gratitude, dedication and enthusiasm in our service to God.

The Unchurched

Perhaps half of the population does not go to church, even on Christmas or Easter. I have talked with many unchurched people and have often heard from them that they do not believe in hell. They so often bring up the subject of hell it is obvious to me that the teaching that God will punish people in hell forever is an issue that weighs heavily upon them. It is as if they feel a strong need to make a rebuttal against what they have often heard about the God of eternal damnation. They hope someone will agree with them, and tell them it is not so, that God really is not like that. They seem to instinctively know God would not throw some people into hell and leave them there for eternity. Consequently, they reject the idea of hell, and sometimes they reject God as well. At that point, they are definitely not really interested in going to church. They cannot bring themselves to worship with a congregation and a minister who believe in a God of eternal damnation.

I am aware that there are other reasons why many people do not attend church. But I believe if we let people know God is love, that God wants to save everyone and will surely be successful, it will remove a significant barrier for many people. They could then joyfully come to Christ and the Church and experience the salvation that Christ provides for everyone.

The teaching of universal salvation is a cornerstone of the Church. Once removed and discarded, it has severely weakened, not only the Church, but also the relationship that many people have with God. The theologian Karl Barth affirms this when he says, "I fear that much of the weakness of our Christian witness comes from the fact that we dare not frankly confess the grandeur of God, the victory of Christ, the superiority of the Spirit."[18]

We deny our members power and enthusiasm because we continue teaching eternal damnation. People sense that while the Church claims to have good news, they do not find it to be particularly newsworthy. The teaching that many will be eternally damned tarnishes the good news. The truly good news of the gospel is that Jesus suffered and died for the salvation of everyone, and it is God's will that not one person be lost. That is the kind of news we can get excited about!

It should be readily obvious to all of us why our evangelistic efforts sometimes meet with such limited success. I believe we would be much more effective if we stopped teaching the bad news of eternal damnation, and instead, consistently presented the good news of salvation for all, along with affirming the liberating and transforming power of God's love in this life as well as the next.

Unnecessary Agonizing

It is always painful for us to mourn the death of a loved one. Fearing eternal damnation can make such a loss even worse. As difficult as it may be to lose a person whom everyone considers to be a Christian, it is much more traumatic to deal with the death of one who apparently was not a believer. What results, is a family that agonizes over the thought of a loved one suffering eternal torment because of not having made a decision for Christ before death. What a cruel burden for people to bear. It is absolutely tragic because it is totally unnecessary.

The only way a person can believe in punishment without

end is to believe that God's grace is available only in this lifetime. It is wonderful to accept and experience God's love and grace but that does not always happen in this life. But there is hope because the Scriptures make it clear that God's grace is not limited to this side of the grave. The Psalmist declares, "If I ascend to heaven, you are there; if I make my bed in Sheol, you are there. If I take the wings of the morning and settle at the farthest limits of the sea, even there your hand shall lead me, and your right hand shall hold me fast" (Psalms 139:8-10). Paul is equally positive in proclaiming that nothing, including death, "will be able to separate us from the love of God in Christ Jesus our Lord" (Romans 8:39).

Meaninglessness and Meanness

If we are driven to reject God due to the teaching of eternal damnation, or for any other reason, the world is very much worse off because of it; in the way we treat each other. When people forget about God, they live according to the law of the jungle. Actually, it is worse than the law of the jungle. People have the capacity to become meaner than other animals. We know we will eventually die. If we do not believe in God or the hereafter and we are driven to get everything we want, we know we will have to get it now, before it is too late. The bottom line for Robert Short is, "Meaninglessness makes people mean."[19]

Meaninglessness can also weigh so heavily upon a person it can cause one to cherish the thought of dying. Sadly, that was the case with Samuel Clemens. In the difficulties of the last years of his life, he came to think of death as a friend. As Short says, "Death is the 'gift' that alone can put an end to the insane meaninglessness of life when there is no God."[20] How sad to think in those terms.

Of course, death is sometimes welcomed to end pain and suffering, even by the believer, and in suffering, one may begin to question the existence of God. How fortunate are those who remain confident of the reality of God and realize God is with us in all experiences of life, in pain as well as pleasure.

In a desperate search for meaning and certainty, atheists may even come back to embrace the God of eternal damnation (the only understanding of God they know). They will stay, though, only if they are given an infallible guarantee that God will not throw them into hell. This guarantee can come in forms, such as; an infallible Bible or an infallible church. The problem with this is that those infallible guarantees become people's gods because they are really trusting in them for salvation.

The other alternative in coming back to God, or in coming to God for the first time, is to recognize that the God of eternal damnation is a myth, realizing that Jesus provides salvation for everyone. With that understanding, we are all much more likely to stay with Jesus and relate to him as our Lord and Savior and as the one who gives rich meaning to our lives.

Making the World a Better Place

We all want to make the world a better place, but that's not likely to become a reality as long as we continue to teach that God imposes or enforces endless punishment in hell. The perception of a cruel God produces cruel Christians. Thinking of God as schizophrenic fosters schizophrenic followers. As Short says, "People always tend to resemble the gods they serve. A vindictive God always produces vindictiveness among those he influences."[21]

People aren't necessarily more humane in the way they treat others because they belong to a church. The self-righteous often pass judgment, handily aided by the Bible. If we believe that God is sometimes vengeful, judgmental, unforgiving, and uncaring, it's easy for us to justify exhibiting at times those same characteristics ourselves. On the other hand, if we really believe that God never condones ungodly behavior and are convinced that God is consistently loving, kind and forgiving, we are more likely to always act that way ourselves.

The world can become a much better place when we change our understanding of hell and God. God is not vengeful, but is always loving of everyone. When we really understand that, and fully assimilate it into our minds and hearts, we can then appreciate the preciousness of others. It is in the example of Christ that we find the basis for loving all humans as they really are. We love each other, not because anyone is perfect, but because we learn to love as God loves. When we realize that God loves us in our imperfections, we also can learn to love unconditionally.

Vonnegut cannot seem to bring himself to believe in God, but he does recognize the value of believing. He urges people to "believe in the most ridiculous superstition of all: that humanity is at the center of the universe, the fulfiller or the frustrater of the grandest dreams of Almighty God. If you can believe that, and make others believe it, then there might be hope for us. Human beings might stop treating each other like garbage, might begin to treasure and protect each other instead."[22]

Unfortunately, it is true that when we emphasize the existence of hell with the same force as we do the existence of heaven, there are those of us who are all too ready to populate hell with those deemed unworthy of heaven. After we condemn the obvious ones such as Judas, Hitler and terrorists, why not go on to others that some may find reprehensible? The list could be endless.

All Christians claim to be loving people. But anyone who is willing to mentally consign others to hell and leave them there does not love fully. If we really do love others, isn't it our obligation to hope and work for the salvation of everyone? We should not just hope that God will save everyone eventually, but believe that all are being saved at the present time. We need to ask ourselves whether we are living in a way which reflects that hope to others and will help it become a reality for them.

Persisting in the belief that some folks go to heaven and others go to hell for eternity sometimes results in those who suppose they are saved becoming very judgmental of those whom they perceive to be lost. With self-righteous indignation they may look down on those whom they think did not have the good sense to accept Christ as their Savior. They may also be very critical of those who have a somewhat different understanding of the faith than they do.

That kind of a judgmental attitude does not foster goodwill and brotherhood. Instead, it can cause a person to feel justified in committing all kinds of atrocities. Tragically, over the centuries, some of the most devoutly religious people have been guilty of perpetrating (or at least defending) blatantly unchristian actions, such as; the crucifixion of Jesus, the Inquisition (through which many thousands of "heretics" were killed), other bitter religious persecutions, and numerous wars.

In believing, on the other hand, that Christ has provided salvation for all and that God will ultimately take everyone to heaven, we can view others from a new perspective. We can no longer justify being judgmental, condemning and cruel to others. We will instead feel inclined to relate to everyone else as redeemed children of God, people who are to be respected, considered precious, and treated as one's brothers and sisters.

Loving Our Enemies

With that attitude, our love can extend even to our enemies. We can love our enemies, because God does. We can have unity with our enemies not only because we all have God as our parent, but also because of our common evil. Jesus illustrates God's unconditional love toward everyone by saying that God "makes his sun rise on the evil and on the good, and sends rain on the righteous and on the unrighteous" (Matthew 5:45).

We would like to believe that we are the good and the righteous, but when we are honest with ourselves we know that we are a mixture of good and evil. Because of that, we know that if God was not merciful toward us, we would be lost. That naturally leads to realize that if God loves us with all our evil, then God must treat our enemies the same way. When we are able to acknowledge our own inner shadow, we will naturally become more tolerant of the shadow in others. In other words, when we learn to love the enemy within, we can develop the compassion and understanding we need to love the enemy without.

If we believe that God loves us but hates those whom we hate, that naturally brings a doubt into our minds. We know that a God who is hostile toward others is potentially hostile toward us as well. And we know, better than anyone else, that there is much to justify such hostility.

The good news is that God is not hostile, toward our enemies or us. We are all in the same situation, friends and enemies alike, all accepted and loved by God, all redeemed by God's grace. We are one in our evil and one in our redemption. All of us are brothers and sisters, children of a loving parent. Thanks be to God!

Fear Versus Hope

As I have stated before, some people cling to the idea of an eternal hell out of the fear that teaching otherwise will cause their loved ones to not appreciate the seriousness of hell, only to end up there because of Godless living. Granted, that can happen if people misunderstand. But the teaching of eternal damnation is a much greater danger because it causes countless people to turn against God, often to become atheists. That negatively affects their behavior, which causes them to experience hell. So, ironically, teaching of eternal hell for the unsaved actually causes that which people fear and are trying to prevent.

No one has ever indicated in any way to me that believing God would eventually save everyone has caused him or her to decide to live in an evil way now and accept God later. In reality, just the opposite is true for many. They have already been putting off making a decision for Christ. That is because, even though they know they should make that decision and commitment, they are repelled by the perception of a condemning God. In contrast, when I tell people of the God of universal salvation, they often stop procrastinating and respond very favorably. They immediately, cheerfully, and gratefully accept God into their lives. Why wait when you can experience the joy of salvation right away?

My experience has been that it is only people in the Church who respond negatively to the announcement that God will eventually save everyone, and far from all church people are unreceptive. Actually, they seem to be exclusively people in spiritual stage 2 who respond negatively, and not even all of them. I have never encountered anyone in the spiritual stages 1, 3 or 4 who were not receptive. Indeed, many of them, especially those in stage 4, have already come to believe in universal salvation. People who have questions and doubts about spiritual matters, or who do not feel accepted by the Church or who are seeking spiritual truth beyond organized religion are very receptive. Relieved that someone has challenged the teaching of eternal damnation, they happily receive the hope of salvation for everyone as wonderful, liberating, good news.

Bad News Versus Good News

It is amazing to me that the teaching of universal salvation is perceived by some people to be bad news. They emphatically reject it. But it is good news! In fact, it is the best possible news. How could anything be better? Universal salvation is something to accept and celebrate with unbridled enthusiasm.

Jesus Said, "Let Your Light Shine"

We have good news!!! It is the promise of salvation for everyone. Because it is such good news and is so important, we need to be about the business of sharing it. Let us boldly tell it; to our children, parents, relatives, co-workers, neighbors, friends, enemies, to everyone around the world.

It is not only our responsibility but also a high privilege to spread the good news. We read in 2 Corinthians 5:19; "In Christ God was reconciling the world to himself, not counting their trespasses against them, and entrusting the message of reconciliation to us." In regard to this calling, Robert Short issues the following urgent appeal: "There is too much at stake for Christians to allow themselves to be intimidated by the wrathful self-righteousness of the 'hell' raising gloomy doomies. . . . Therefore, our witness to them should be just as aggressive and unambiguous as theirs has been to us."[23]

If we who believe in universal salvation keep quiet instead of speaking up, the only message that people will hear is the untrue and incredibly bad news of eternal damnation. We must not be intimidated into silence, but freely spread the good news. Salvation is complete. Karl Barth says, "The task of the church is to announce the good news of the perfect work of Christ done for all. . . . The distinction is not between redeemed and non-redeemed, but between those who realize it and those who do not."[24]

May we help others realize and experience the salvation that Christ has provided for all of us.

Appendix

SILENCE IS NOT GOLDEN

A Handbook on Spreading the Wonderful News of Salvation for Everyone

If you want to tell others the good news of universal salvation but wonder how you can best do that, please read on. I will share with you how you might effectively share the news of salvation with others, what you can expect to happen when you do, and how you can utilize people's reactions (positive or negative) to help further the cause.

It is important to realize we are not on our own in our endeavor to carry out this great calling from God. We are privileged to be a part of God's plan of salvation. Through it all, God is with us. It is very helpful to spend much time in prayer, to seek God's guidance and inspiration, to be Christ-like in all situations, to be patient, loving, kind, forgiving, understanding, supportive, and Spirit-led. We also need to pray for others, that they may be receptive to all God has to offer them.

It is also very important that we who believe in universal salvation support each other. Others of like mind and spirit can help us maintain a positive attitude even if people do not always respond as favorably as we would like. Do not be discouraged if you do not already have Universalist friends. It is usually not difficult to find people for that kind of support group because some people already believe in universal salvation and many others are receptive to it. Besides, you will discover that often a very strong bond quickly develops between you and others who believe in salvation for everyone.

There are some churches that officially endorse universal salvation, and some in which the minister or others promote it even though it is contrary to their church's official doctrine, but they are not easy to find. Do not let that discourage you. You can effectively promote universalism in and through churches where there is overall receptivity to the teaching, as well as with churches where there is opposition to universalism among the members. You also can promote it very effectively outside of the Church.

Sharing this book with others is a very effective means of spreading the news of universal salvation. Just as you might enthusiastically tell a friend or acquaintance about any other book you have read, you can tell them of this book. You can offer to loan it to them. Better yet, keep a few copies of the book on hand so you can give them as gifts. Then the recipients can keep the books for future reference and to loan to other people.

It is also very helpful to utilize the companion to this book, a study book of the same title. It consists of thirteen lessons with study/discussion questions at the end of each lesson. The Study Book is intended for use with youth or adult Sunday School classes or other groups of church members. It can also be used for a non-church study group in your home.

Responses You Can Expect

Unchurched people are usually very receptive to the belief that God will eventually succeed in saving everyone. Often the reason they are unchurched is because they have been driven from the Church by the teaching of a judgmental God. So they almost always receive universalism as wonderful, liberating good news.

Many people who attend church are also quite receptive to universal salvation. In contrast to the unchurched, however, church members' responses fall along the entire spectrum from enthusiastically positive to extremely negative. Their responses make life very interesting.

Some people already staunchly believe that God will eventually save everyone, and are well versed in the theological reasons why it is so. Others, who are not as confident, believe in universalism but they may not know that the belief is theologically well founded. They are among those who may have arrived at the conclusion more out of instinct than theological training. Most people who believe in universalism do not know that there are many others who believe the same way. Because of that, when you share your views with them, they will often embrace you with open arms out of appreciation that someone has finally expressed what they believe. They will be delighted to find in you a kindred spirit.

Many people have never heard of the concept of universal salvation and have not thought of it as a possibility. Not knowing better, they are ones who have been carrying with them the burden of the perception of a wrathful, judgmental God. Upon being told in a way that is convincing enough to overcome perhaps life-long negative indoctrination regarding God, they receive the news of salvation for everyone as a breath of fresh air. Upon realizing that God is really loving, forgiving and saving of everyone, they begin to celebrate the good news. They are delighted to be liberated.

Some people receive the news of universal salvation in a thoughtful way. They find it interesting, but it is a new idea to them and they are not convinced of its truth. While they are not ready to embrace universalism, they support your right to believe it. Others disagree with the idea that God will eventually save everyone. They believe that those who hold to the belief are wrong, but they tolerate you as one who does believe it, and perhaps will agree to disagree. A few people (primarily fundamentalist Christians) take very strong exception to the teaching of universalism, and tell you how wrong they think you are.

The first thing we need to affirm regarding the various responses to universal salvation is that each person is where he or she needs to be at that time on their spiritual journey. Where they are is all right with God and should be with us as well.

It is also good to keep in mind that the teaching of universalism is a new idea to most people. It is not realistic to expect everyone to embrace it immediately because they often have deeply ingrained and long-standing beliefs to the contrary. With some time and further thought, however, many of the ones who initially respond with skepticism and negativity will eventually come to believe in universal salvation.

Utilizing Opposition

It is very helpful to realize that the small numbers of people who respond most negatively are in reality your co-workers in spreading the good news of salvation for everyone. Of course, they do not realize they are helping you through their criticism of you. Also, because of the pain they can sometimes inflict upon you, it may take considerable time and graciousness on your part before you are able to realize and fully appreciate how helpful they are to the cause of spreading universalism.

The reason the critics are so helpful is because they often tell others about your beliefs and how misguided they think you are. That creates enough of a stir that an ever-increasing number of people begin to talk about it. As the word spreads through the controversy, other people wonder what the fuss is all about. That motivates them to find out more about universalism. Upon learning about universal salvation and why it is so important, the majority of those people are very receptive to it. Some of the new adherents to universalism become strong proponents of the teaching, and proceed to freely tell others about it. That generates more controversy, which results in further spreading the good news of salvation for everyone, and so on.

Let us not forget that, while it is much more pleasant and enjoyable to speak of universal salvation to those who happily receive it, it is often through controversy that the news of universalism is most effectively spread. The natural tendency for most of us is to shy away from controversy and to avoid negative responses from others if at all possible. The key thing we need to remember in this regard is that if we timidly try to avoid unpleasant reactions from others, we will probably end up not saying anything to anyone about universal salvation, and those who promote doom and gloom will continue to prevail. But if we are courageous enough to not only endure some negative reactions from a few people, but also utilize it, we can make a powerful difference in the lives of countless people who yearn for good news.

I'm well aware that it is especially risky for clergy to promote the teaching of universal salvation. Most ministers serve churches in denominations that officially adhere to the teaching of everlasting punishment in hell for the unsaved. If ministers of those churches promote universalism, they run the risk of encountering significant opposition from a few of their church members.

In my contacts with other ministers, I have found that a major percentage of them believe in universal salvation but most of them never teach it or even openly admit it to their parishioners. They are afraid of losing their jobs. I can understand that. I did the same thing for many years. I will always remember the first sermon I preached on the subject of universalism. I naively thought everyone would think it was wonderful and exciting good news, and respond favorably. Most people did, but a few very negative outspoken ones did not. I didn't have the courage to speak of it again for years.

Having been intimidated into silence, while knowing I should speak up, kept eating at me over time, and I have finally gotten to the place where I can no longer keep quiet. There is too much at stake to bow to intimidation. It is a small, although loud and intimidating, minority of people who have in the past prevented the spread of universalism. The rest of us have been intimidated into letting them do it. No more!

The good news is that there is no reason for us to be intimidated. The bark of those in opposition is much worse than their bite. Besides, they are a small minority. Most people respond favorably, so we can feel free to stand up and be counted, to faithfully spread the wonderful news about God's unconditional love, unlimited power, undying grace, unmerited favor; God's salvation for everyone.

Hopefulness Through Faithful Leadership

It saddens me to recognize that, because of the risk to them, we probably cannot rely on the clergy to lead in this great movement. If we are going to be successful within the churches in our endeavor to spread the wonderful news of salvation for everyone, lay members will probably have to take the primary responsibility to carry the banner. They have a great advantage over the clergy in that they do not run the risk of getting fired. They, just as the clergy, however, are sometimes subjected to the same negative reactions from those who oppose the teaching of universalism. I encourage those of you who are laity to muster the necessary courage and faithfulness to overcome that opposition. If you take the lead and pave the way, many of your ministers will eventually realize it is safe, and will openly join you in the cause.

I want you to know that, while you may lose a few church members if you proclaim the good news of salvation for everyone, there will be many, many others who will come into the church specifically because of your stand.

It appears to me that perhaps the greatest hope for spreading the news of universal salvation could take place outside of the Church, as a grass-roots movement. There is virtually no opposition to the teaching among the unchurched. People outside the Church have no turf to defend. There is no worry of offending other church members. They also do not have to overcome the co-dependence that often exists in churches.

I realize it may seem perplexing to many people that those who do not attend church could lead a spiritual movement. But let us give that some more thought. While many people find church participation to be extremely helpful to them on their spiritual journey, surely we can all agree that it is not necessary to go to church in order to be a Christian or to be spiritually mature. I have met many unchurched people who have the Spirit of Christ in them and are very advanced spiritually. They are well qualified to lead in the cause of universalism.

In order to experience the greatest possible success in our efforts to spread the news of salvation for everyone through Christ, all of us who believe in it will need to do our part; clergy and lay church members, as well as those who are outside the Church.

The Blessing of Persecution

Let us take Matthew 5:11-12 as our Scriptural theme; "Blessed are you when people revile you and persecute you and utter all kinds of evil against you falsely on my account. Rejoice and be glad, for your reward is great in heaven, for in the same way they persecuted the prophets who were before you." Not only does the experience of persecution put us in very good company (with the prophets and Jesus), but also it is precisely through persecution and controversy that the belief in universalism is spread.

The opponents of the teaching that Christ has provided salvation for everyone cannot squash the movement today like they did in the sixth century. We enjoy much greater freedom (of religion, press, etc.), and have the benefits of the mass media and instant communications. The Church does not exercise total control anymore. The threat of excommunication falls on deaf ears.

Christianity has always flourished in the midst of adversity. It is well known that such was the case during the first several decades following the time of Christ. The same principle applies to spreading the news of universal salvation. In the late eighteenth and early nineteenth century in the United States, the Universalist movement encountered significant opposition but rose to its greatest strength in modern times. In spite of persecution, or because of it, the Universalists grew rapidly in numbers, reaching several hundred thousand adherents in the United States by 1850.

Sadly, the organized Universalist movement declined substantially during the twentieth century. But the cause is not lost. It is a new day and God's Spirit is moving in our midst. People are spiritually hungry for good news. A growing number of people are coming to believe in universal salvation and to freely share it with others.

If we follow the example of the early Universalists in boldly and broadly proclaiming the good news of salvation for everyone, and are willing to endure some opposition, the Universalist cause will again grow to a mighty movement. This will take place, not only in spite of persecution, but also because of it. We will restore the belief to prominence, as it was during the first centuries of the Christian Church.

And we will rejoice and be glad.

NOTES

CHAPTER ONE: DARE TO POSSESS THE TRUTH: What Does the Bible Say Regarding Universal Salvation?

1. Robert Young, *Analytical Concordance to the Bible* Grand Rapids: William B. Eerdman's Publishing Company, 1970), p. 308.
2. Ibid., pp. 308, 310-311.
3. *The Columbian Congress of the Universalist Church* (Boston: Universalist Publishing House, 1883), p. 147. Also: John Wesley Hanson, *Aion-Aionios: the Greek Word Translated Everlasting—Eternal, in the Holy Bible, Shown to Denote Limited Duration* (Chicago: North-western Universalist Publishing House, 1876), pp. 72-75.
4. *An Intermediate Greek-English Lexicon* (Oxford: Clarendon Press, first edition 1889, Impression 1968), p. 25.
5. Young, pp. 308, 310.
6. William Barclay, *The Mind of Jesus* (New York: Harper & Row Publishers, 1960), p. 280.
7. *The Interpreter's Bible: A Commentary in Twelve Volumes*, Vol. 11 (Nashville: Abingdon Press, 1955), p. 51.

CHAPTER TWO: SEEING THE BIGGER PICTURE: General Biblical Themes

1. Raymond A. Moody Jr., *Life After Life* (New York: Bantam Books, 1975), p. 59.
2. Raymond A. Moody Jr., *Reflections on Life After Life* (New York: Bantam Books, 1977), p. 32.
3. David Lowes Watson, *God Does Not Foreclose: The Universal Promise of Salvation* (Nashville: Abingdon Press, 1990), p. 90.

4. Maurice Rawlings, *Beyond Death's Door* (New York: Bantam Books, 1978), pp. 87-88.

CHAPTER THREE: AMAZING GRACE: Implications of Universal Salvation Versus Eternal Damnation

1. L. A. King, "Hell, the Painful Refuge", *Eternity Magazine*, January 1979, p. 29.
2. Karl Barth, *Church Dogmatics*, Vol. 2, Part 2, (Edinburgh: T. & T. Clark, 1957), pp. 449-450.
3. Leslie D. Weatherhead, *Life Begins at Death* (Nashville: Abingdon Press, 1969), p. 67.

CHAPTER FOUR: I WANT TO DO IT MYSELF: Do We Have Free Will?

1. Robert Short, *Something To Believe In* (New York: Harper & Row Publishers, 1978), p. 250.
2. *Martin Luther: Selections From His Writings*, Ed. John Dillenberger (New York: Garden City, 1961), p. 199.
3. Short, p. 54.
4. Ibid.
5. *The Works of John Wesley*, Vol. 2, Sermons 34-70, Ed. Albert C. Outler, (Nashville: Abingdon Press, 1985), p. 490.

CHAPTER FIVE: LAYING A SOLID FOUNDATION: What God Is Like

1. C.S. Lewis, *Mere Christianity* (New York: Simon & Schuster, 1980), pp. 153-154.
2. Paul Tillich, *Systematic Theology*, Vol. 2 (Chicago: The University of Chicago Press, 1957), p. 7.
3. Ernst Feil, *The Theology of Dietrich Bonhoeffer*, Trans. Martin Rumscheidt (Philadelphia: Fortress Press, 1985), p. 91.

4. M. Scott Peck, *The Road Less Traveled* (New York: Simon and Schuster, 1978), p. 281.
5. Matthew Fox, *Original Blessing* (Santa Fe: Bear & Company, 1983), p. 90.
6. L. Robert Keck, *Sacred Eyes* (Boulder: Synergy Associates, Inc., 1992), p. 49.

CHAPTER SIX: FREE AT LAST: From Hell to Heaven-How it Is Accomplished

1. Leslie Weatherhead, *When the Lamp Flickers* (Nashville: Abingdon – Cokesbury Press, 1948), p. 185.
2. Peck, p. 273.
3. Ibid., p. 277.
4. Walter Wink, *Engaging the Powers* (Minneapolis: Fortress Press, 1992), p. 268.

CHAPTER SEVEN: GOING BEYOND WISHFUL THINKING: The Power of Unconditional Love

1. Melody Beattie, *The Language of Letting Go* (Center City, MN: Hazelden Foundation,1990), pp. 144, 145.
2. Ibid., p. 95.
3. Marianne Williamson, *A Return To Love* (New York: HarperCollins Publishers, 1992), p. 160.

CHAPTER EIGHT: FORGIVENESS IS ONLY THE BEGINNING: Growing into God's Likeness

1. Williston Walker, *A History of the Christian Church* (New York: Charles Scribner's Sons, 1970), p. 51.
2. M. Scott Peck, *Further Along The Road Less Traveled* (New York: Simon & Schuster, 1993), pp. 120-131.
3. Weatherhead, *Life Begins at Death*, p. 13.

CHAPTER NINE: MISERY LOVES COMPANY: Why Some People Cling to the Idea of Eternal Damnation

1. Karl Barth, *God Here and Now*, Trans. Paul M. Van Buren (New York: Harper & Row Publishers, 1964), p. 33.
2. Anne Wilson Schaef, *Co-dependence Misunderstood Mistreated* (San Francisco: HarperCollins Publishers, 1986), p. 50.
3. Walker, p. 296.
4. *The United Methodist Hymnal* (Nashville: The United Methodist Publishing House, 1989), p. 45.

CHAPTER TEN: THE ANCIENTS HAVE STOLEN OUR BEST IDEAS: The History of Universalism

1. Columbian Congress, p. 147.
2. Ibid., p. 158.
3. Ibid., p. 150.
4. Ibid., p. 151.
5. Ibid., p. 154.
6. Ibid.
7. Ibid., p. 170.
8. Origen, *On First Principals*, Trans. G. W. Butterworth (New York: Harper & Row, Publishers, 1966), p. 146.
9. Walker, p. 64.
10. Joseph W. Trigg, *Origen: The Bible and Philosophy in the Third-Century Church* (Atlanta: John Knox Press, 1983), p. 114.
11. Columbian Congress, p. 158. Also: Hanson, p. 71.
12. Columbian Congress, pp. 147-148.
13. Ibid., p. 147.
14. Ibid., p. 159.
15. Brian E. Daley, *The Hope of the Early Church: A Handbook of Patristic Eschatology* (Cambridge: Cambridge University Press, 1991), p. 85.
16. Ibid., pp. 87, 89.
17. Ibid., p. 97.

18. Ibid.
19. Ibid., p. 99.
20. Walker, pp. 158-159.
21. Daley, pp. 101, 103.
22. Walker, pp. 160-162.
23. Daley, p. 138.
24. Ibid., p. 139.
25. Ibid.
26. Ibid.
27. Ibid., p. 140.
28. *The Fathers of the Church, Vol. 24, Saint Augustine, The City of God*, Trans. Gerald G. Walsh and Daniel J. Donan (Washington, D. C.: The Catholic University of America Press, 1954), p. 365.
29. Ibid., p. 248.
30. Ibid., pp. 378-379.
31. Ibid., p. 391.
32. Daley, pp. 188, 189, 190.
33. Ibid., p. 189.; Also Hanson, p. 74.
34. Hanson, p. 73.
35. Ibid., p. 74.
36. Ibid.
37. Columbian Congress, p. 174.
38. *John Wesley's Forty-Four Sermons* (London: Epworth Press, 1944), p. 4.
39. *The Journal of the Rev. John Wesley, A. M.*, Standard Edition, Vol. II, Ed. Nehemiah Curnock (London: Charles H. Kelly, 1909-1916), p. 498.
40. Ibid.
41. *The Works of John Wesley*, Vol. 2, pp. 400, 410, 411.
42. *Colliers Encyclopedia*, Vol. 22 (Crowell-Collier Educational Corporation, 1969), p. 741.
43. Ibid.
44. Russell E. Miller, *The Larger Hope: The First Century of the Universalist Church in America, 1770-1870* (Boston: Unitarian Universalist Association, 1979), pp. 11-12.
45. Ibid., pp. 13-33.

46. Ibid., p. 21.
47. Ibid., p. 741.
48. Hosea Ballou, *A Treatise on Atonement* (Boston: The Universalist Publishing House, 1902), p. 222.
49. Ernest Cassara, *Hosea Ballou; The Challenge to Orthodoxy* (Boston: Universalist Historical Society and Beacon Press, 1961), pp. 151, 167.
50. *The Unitarian Universalist Pocket Guide*, Ed. William F. Schulz (Boston: Skinner House Books, 1993), p. 89.
51. A. Boyce Gibson, *The Religion of Dostoevsky* (Philadelphia: Westminster Press, 1973), pp. 180, 201.
52. Friedrich Schleiermacher, *The Christian Faith* (Edinburgh: T. & T. Clark, 1948), pp. 720, 722.
53. Dietrich Bonhoeffer, *Ethics*, Ed. Eberhard Bethge (New York: The Macmillan Company, 1945), pp. 70-71.
54. Barth, *Church Dogmatics*, p. 306.
55. Paul Tillich, *The Eternal Now* (New York: Charles Scribner's Sons, 1963), p. 121.
56. Paul Tillich, *Systematic Theology*, Vol. 3 (Chicago: The University of Chicago Press, 1963), p. 408.

CHAPTER ELEVEN: MAKING MOUNTAINS OUT OF MOUNTAINS: The Significance of This Issue

1. Mark Twain, *The Mysterious Stranger* (New York: Harper & Brothers Publishers, 1916), pp. 150-151.
2. Mark Twain, *What is Man?*, Ed. Paul Baender (Berkeley: University of California Press, 1973), pp. 56-57.
3. Short, p. 90.
4. Twain, *What is Man?*, p. 399.
5. Bertrand Russell, *Why I Am Not A Christian*, Ed. Paul Edwards (New York: Simon and Schuster, 1957), pp. 17, 18.
6. Ibid., p. 35.
7. Ruth Hurmence Green, *The Born Again Skeptic's Guide to the Bible* (Madison: Freedom From Religion Foundation, 1979), p. vii.

8. Ibid., pp. 19, 34.
9. Short, p. 88.
10. Kurt Vonnegut, *Wampeters, Foma & Granfalloons* (New York: Delacorte/Seymour Lawrence, 1974), p. 162.
11. Ibid.
12. Anton Szander LaVey, *The Satanic Bible* (New York: Avon Books, 1969), p. 61.
13. Ibid., p. 55.
14. Ibid., p. 62.
15. Ibid., p. 86.
16. Ibid., p. 54.
17. Short, p. 47.
18. Karl Barth, *The Faith of the Church* (New York: Meridian Books, Inc., 1958), p. 173.
19. Short, p. 123.
20. Ibid., p. 152.
21. Ibid., p. 253.
22. Vonnegut, pp. 163-164.
23. Short, p. 281.
24. John Godsey, Ed., *Karl Barth's Table Talk* (Richmond: John Knox Press, 1962), p. 87.